BEYOND

simple words

THE BROKEN

at sacred edges

LIGHTS

To
Marcia, Joshua, and Maria
and to the
Northminster Baptist Church,
our family's family of faith

CHARLES E. POOLE

BEYOND

simple words

THE BROKEN

at sacred edges

LIGHTS

SMYTH&HELWYS
PUBLISHING INCORPORATED   MACON, GEORGIA
WWW.HELWYS.COM

SMYTH&
HELWYS

Smyth & Helwys Publishing, Inc.
6316 Peake Road
Macon, Georgia 31210-3960
1-800-747-3016
©2000 by Smyth & Helwys Publishing
All rights reserved.
Printed in the United States of America.

Charles E. Poole

All biblical quotations are taken from the New Revised Standard
Version (NRSV) unless otherwise indicated.

Library of Congress Cataloging-in-Publication Data

Poole, Charles E.
    Beyond the broken lights: simple words at sacred edges
    p.   cm.   (alk. paper)
    Includes bibliographical references.
    1. Christian life—Baptist authors. I. Title.
    BV4510.2.P66   2000
    248'.4'861—dc21   99-38655
                                                     CIP
ISBN 978-1-57312-270-2

CONTENTS

PREFACE

Theodore Adams once told about a preacher who, when asked, "How long does it take to prepare a sermon?" replied, "All my life up to now." I suppose that is true of all efforts to say whatever we sense to be so about God and life. It has certainly taken me "all my life up to now" to hammer out the words that rest inside this book. All my life up to now I have had the blessing of family, friends, and teachers alongside whom I have struggled to glimpse something of the gospel of God. My debts run deep and go all the way back to childhood and home . . . to mother, father, and my sister Rhonda.

I am grateful to the folks at Smyth and Helwys for bringing these words to the light of day. The year 2000 will mark the company's tenth anniversary of faithful service to believers and seekers across the nation and across the seas. It has been a joy to watch their vision take shape and touch lives for good. Of their many outstanding people, Jackie Riley is the editor who has worked most closely with these words. I am grateful to Jackie for her editorial insight and to Shirley Sanders Reid whose diligent and patient typing rendered my handwritten words into a form that Editor Riley could read.

I often find myself going back to William Butler Yeats' observation that out of our quarrels with others we make rhetoric, but out of our quarrels with ourselves we make poetry. Translated into matters of the Spirit, it seems to me that out of our quarrels with others, we take up positions, but out of our quarrels with ourselves, we whisper quiet confessions of faith.

I have never cared for theological quarrels with others, but inside my soul I carry on a perpetual, quiet quarrel with myself concerning the great mysteries of God and life. The leftovers of that quiet internal quarrel have found their way onto these pages as quiet confessions that lean toward a "simple gospel" approach to God and life. In his wonderful biography of the great Quaker, Douglas Steere, Glenn Hinson quotes Steere as saying, "There are deeps in all of us far below our ideas." I have sought to be honest to those "deeps that lie deeper than ideas" in my own soul and to bear witness to them in these pages.

The words that have found a home in this book are dedicated to Marcia, Joshua, and Maria; such light and joy they bring to life. No words can tell my thanksgiving for their grace . . . and to Northminster Baptist Church, our family's family of faith, a remarkable congregation for which we say, "Thanks be to God."

—Charles Poole
Jackson, Mississippi
Easter 1999

BEYOND THE BROKEN LIGHTS

There is a place where words run out. That may seem an odd place to begin a book that has only more words to offer, but it is a fact, and we may as well face it. When it comes to defining, describing, and pondering the ways of God, it is especially evident that there is, indeed, a silent, quiet, speechless place where words run out, a point beyond which words cannot go. No one has ever better described the place where words run out than T. S. Eliot:

> Words strain,
> Crack and sometimes break, under the burden.
> Under the tension, slip, slide, perish . . .
> Will not stay in place, will not stay still
> . . . So here I am, in the middle way, having had twenty years
> Twenty years largely wasted . . .
> Trying to learn to use words, and every attempt
> Is a wholly new start and a different kind of failure.
> Because one has only learnt to get the better of words
> For the thing one no longer has to say . . .[1]

When it comes to the gospel of God, it is just as Eliot said. Every attempt at explaining, defining, and corralling the ways of God is "a different kind of failure." Our words about God, the words we stack high into doctrines, creeds, and confessions are helpful, illuminating, even necessary and indispensable to our shared lives as believers. But those words, wonderful as they are, "strain, crack, and sometimes break" beneath the enormous, magnificent, finally unspeakable weight of the glory and wonder of God.

And yet, we have to try. We must make our attempts. But we must also remember that, when it comes to the truth about God, "something breaks through language and escapes."[2] Perhaps that is what Isaiah had in mind when he said, "'For my thoughts are not your thoughts, nor are your ways my ways,' says the Lord" (55:8). Perhaps that is what Paul had in mind when he wrote, "How unsearchable are [God's] judgments and how inscrutable [God's] ways! For who has known the mind of the Lord?" (Rom 11:33b-34a). Perhaps that is what Alfred Tennyson sought to say with his unforgettable verse:

> Our little systems have their day
> They have their day and cease to be
> They are but broken lights of Thee
> And Thou, O Lord, art more than they.[3]

By the time Tennyson wrote those words, he had lived through the darkness of his best friend's untimely death. Tennyson had struggled to understand. He had yearned for clarity in the depths of mystery. And, though Tennyson found no satisfactory explanations, no complete resolutions, no simple, take-it-or-leave-it answers, he did emerge from the darkness to say a profound word of truth: All our "little systems," our systems of theological position and conventional wisdom and standard orthodoxy, have their day and then cease to be. They are, Tennyson said, "broken lights":

> They are but broken lights of Thee
> And Thou, O Lord, art more than they.

Broken lights are certainly better than no lights at all. Indeed, since there are no other lights—no perfect, seamless, unbroken lights that human words can shine on sacred truth—the broken lights are precious to us. We love our systems of traditional orthodoxy and conventional wisdom. They are the lights by which we live. We would not know how to live without them. We could do worse than live by those familiar lights of religious tradition. Perhaps, in this life, we can do no better. However, we sometimes must remind ourselves that all our theological systems are broken lights: limited, flawed, unfinished lights. That includes what Augustine said, what Calvin said, what Luther said, what Zwingli said, what E. Y. Mullins and Karl Barth and Paul Tillich said. . . Every theory of the atonement, every denominational platform— the reformed tradition, the Baptist principles, the Papal announcements—all are broken lights. We hold to them because they are the only lights we have by which to stumble around the sacred edges. We need them. They help us. But we must not clutch them too tightly, lest we cut ourselves on them, and we must not wave them about too zealously, lest we injure someone, because all of them are broken lights.

Beyond them, somewhere past the last margin of their flickering, shimmering, well-intentioned beams, there is God. And God, as Tennyson so rightly surmised, is more than all the little systems and broken lights combined can tell or reveal or corral or say. Our systems of standard orthodoxy and conventional wisdom do have a purpose to serve and a role to fill; they "have their day." But their day will pass. They will cease to be because they are but broken lights, and the truth about God and life is deeper, higher, and wider than all our tries at the truth can confess. There is truth not yet glimpsed. It is the rest of the truth about God and life, the truth that waits beyond the broken lights, somewhere past the place where words run out.

The truth that waits *beyond* the broken lights is the same truth that was *before* the broken lights. Before all our little systems began having their day, there was the truth about God and life. The words that wait their turn inside this book yearn to recover something that was *before* the broken lights, and they long to glimpse something that is *beyond* the broken lights. Alas, they are certain to fail. They cannot reach back that far or reach up that high. But that does not keep them from trying. They have to try. Like all human words that hunger to taste and tell that which is sacred, they are only hesitant tries for the truth that was before, and is beyond, the broken lights. As such, I suppose they are, themselves, just little slivers of broken light, swept up on the paper altar where now they take their turn, stammering their tries at the truth, in a whisper from the edges of God.

NEW LIGHT

One of the more memorable song titles of recent years belongs to a ballad called "The Trouble with the Truth." Sung by the famous twentieth-century American poet Patty Loveless, "The Trouble with the Truth" is all about how demanding the truth can be.[4] The trouble with the truth is that, once we see it and know it, it might demand more of us than we can comfortably give. That is sort of what the song suggests. The song is not wrong. As one wise theologian once said, "The truth will make you free, but before it makes you free, it will make you mad."[5] That is the trouble with the truth.

Jesus was certainly familiar with the trouble with the truth. He revealed more of the truth about God than anyone had ever before seen. And it was for that reason—because he cast new light on the truth about God—that he was always in such trouble. The conflict that surrounded Jesus was usually related to the trouble that too much truth caused people who didn't want to be troubled by the truth.

The Pharisees were troubled by the truth that Jesus was bringing out into the light. Jesus was throwing too much light on too much truth, and the Pharisees weren't interested in following new light to new places. They had found a familiar place to stand.

The last thing they needed was a new road to walk. So, when Jesus began to cast new light on the truth about who God is, how God acts, and what God wants, the Pharisees became angry.

The dispute over new light can be overheard in Luke 5 and 6. In Luke 5:17-26 Jesus is confronted by the Pharisees for promising forgiveness to a sinner. Then, in Luke 5:27-32, he is in trouble with the Pharisees for sharing a dinner with a sinner. Skip forward to Luke 6:1-5, and the Pharisees are fussing at Jesus for picking a little snack from a grainfield on the Sabbath, and then, in Luke 6:6-11, the Pharisees ambush Jesus again, this time for healing on the Sabbath. At the center of all this conflict and controversy the Pharisees imply that Jesus is less religious than they because he and his followers are always eating and drinking rather than fasting. In response, Jesus told the parable about new wine bursting old wineskins. Throughout this section of Luke's Gospel, the Pharisees are asking Jesus one basic, simple, enormous question: "What gives you the right to relate to God and people in ways that are different from what we have always believed?" In this "controversy section" of Luke's Gospel, the Pharisees want to know why Jesus breaks their rules by picking a few plums on the Sabbath, why Jesus defies their tradition by healing on the Sabbath, why Jesus colors outside their lines by eating with known sinners, and why Jesus ignores their scrupulous schedule for fasting. If you add it all up, the sum total of their many questions equals one huge question: "What gives you the right to relate to God and people in ways that are different from what we have always believed?" That is the Pharisees' question for Jesus.

Now, right about here, we should probably string a caution light across our path because it is usually right about here that we tend to start indicting the Pharisees. When we start wandering around inside these "conflict sections" of the Gospels and we

keep bumping into these frustrated, angry, confrontational Pharisees ambushing Jesus, our tendency is to assail the Pharisees.
That's why we need a blinking yellow caution light right about
here to slow us down.

Put yourself in the Pharisees' place. The Pharisees were not
bad people. Most of the Pharisees were sincerely committed to a
life of careful interpretation of, and obedience to, the Law. The
Pharisees were laypersons, not professional priests. They were
not scholars, as were the scribes. Rather, they were people whose
chief commitment was to obeying and preserving the Law of God
as it was interpreted by the scribes. The scribes were responsible
for articulating much of the legalistic traditions that grew up like
a fence around the Law, and the Pharisees were the ones who
were most committed to obeying those traditions and convincing
others to do the same.[6] Thus, it is not difficult to understand their
frustration with Jesus.

When Jesus ate with sinners or healed someone on the
Sabbath or something like that, it angered the Pharisees and,
probably, frightened them. They had a lot of life invested in some
traditional interpretations of the Law, and Jesus was relating to
God and people in ways that transcended those traditional interpretations. That doesn't mean the Pharisees were evil; it just
means they were a lot like you and me. When new light pre-
sented the Pharisees with new ways of thinking about the truth,
it was troubling to them. Jesus was relating to God's law and
God's people in ways that were different from what the Pharisees
had always been taught. He was not fasting as often as they
fasted. He was doing things on the Sabbath that they had always
thought the Law prohibited. Jesus was casting new light on old
truth, and the Pharisees were troubled.

Which is probably why Jesus told them the little story about
new wine bursting old skins. Old leather wineskins grew brittle

and rigid with age. If one were to put new, fermenting wine into rigid, inflexible old containers, the fermentation of the new wine would cause the old skins to rip at the seams. New wine had to go into flexible new wineskins. On one level, that is what Jesus' little story was about—new wine bursting old skins. But, that, of course, is not what the story was really about.

Jesus wasn't really talking about new wine and old skins. What he was really talking about was new light on old truth. Jesus was telling the Pharisees that their old wineskins of opinion and tradition would not accommodate the new wine of the gospel the Jesus was preaching and teaching and living. Jesus was inviting them to put down some of their comfortable old opinions and to take up some new wineskins, new ways of thinking and acting that would be nearer to the truth about God, the truth that Jesus was bringing out into a fuller, brighter, clearer light than ever the world had seen.

Jesus wasn't bringing new truth. What had always been true about God was still true about God. Jesus was bringing new light on the old truth and revealing more of the truth about God than anyone had ever before seen. The words and works of Jesus constituted the best look the world has ever had at who God is, how God acts, and what God wants. Jesus brought new light to bear upon the truth about God, and he called people to follow that new light, change their mind if new light demanded it, and go forward into the fullest and best revelation of God they had seen. Jesus called people to be honest with new light, put down old wineskins of opinion, and let their minds and lives be changed by new light on old truth.

Does all this talk of new wine bursting old skins and new light revealing old truth suggest that every new idea is a good idea? Does all of this mean that to follow Jesus is to summarily discard old ideas and to indiscriminately embrace new ideas? Of course not. After all, some new notions are dreadful, and some old ideas are wonderful. What we are after is not whatever is most new, but whatever is most true. The honest, open, unencumbered quest for the truth will sometimes require us to follow new light to new places, and that same quest for the truth will sometimes require us to reaffirm familiar convictions and renew our commitments to old ideas. The real issue is never about new or old. The issue, rather, is about learning, as best we can, the truth of the gospel and then conforming our lives to it; following new light on God's truth, wherever it leads.

That, of course, can be bothersome, because if we are honest with new light and follow it, we might actually have to change our ways—what Jesus called "putting down old wineskins and taking up new ones." It can be painful to set aside comfortable, familiar ideas about God and life and embrace new light that might cause us to have to change our ways. That is not easy, which I suspect is why at the end of the parable Jesus said, "No one, after drinking old wine desires new wine." In other words, "Who wants to be bothered with new light and more insight on God's truth? After all, if we see new light, if we learn more of the truth about God, we might have to change the way we live or act or talk."

That's what Jesus meant, I suspect, with his footnote to the parable: "People aren't very interested in new wine. They like the old, familiar, comfortable wine that doesn't demand any change in their lives." Sort of like a T-shirt I once saw hanging in a gift shop. On the front of the T-shirt, in huge, bold, emphatic type were the words, "**CHANGE IS GOOD**." Then down below, in little tiny letters, were the words, "You go first." The T-shirt captured the story. Change is good, just so I'm not the one being changed. But if I honestly embrace the new light that our Lord Jesus brings to bear on God's truth, then I will be changed. I will have to change in order to conform my life to the truth I have seen.

A verse in 2 Peter admonishes us to "grow in grace and in the knowledge of our Lord and Savior Jesus Christ." But a person cannot grow without changing. To grow in grace and in the knowledge of our Lord and Savior Jesus Christ will require of us changes in the way we speak and live and act. The change can be painful, but beyond the growing pain of the changing there is the joy of knowing that we have been true to the new light we have seen.

I am no stranger to this painful business of putting down old wineskins and taking up new ones. In the past I have had to let new light on old truth change my life, and I suspect I will again as life continues to unfold. For example, I once thought that only men should be ministers, but as I began to interpret the whole Bible in the light of the life of our Lord Jesus, I began to see that I could not square my tightly-held notions of gender-exclusion with the spirit of Christ. I began to see that I was wrong. So, what could I do?

Well, first I got angry at those who had shown me the new light because the new light was forcing me to struggle with something I had already settled. Then I felt guilty for seeing the new light because I thought that believing something different than what I had always believed meant that I was ungrateful for my roots. So, for a long time I didn't let on. I knew better than I would admit. But, finally, I reached the place at which I knew that I had to deny the new light I had seen or follow the new light and say out loud that a Christ-centered interpretation of the whole New Testament had caused me to set aside my old wineskin of exclusion and take up a new wineskin of conviction that God can call whomever God wants to, to do whatever God wants them to do, without regard for their gender. (I'm sure God was greatly relieved to have my permission!) It all sounds so simple now. But at the time it was a painful, difficult, wineskin-bursting change in my life.

That's just one example of the pain and joy of putting down old wineskins and taking up new ones. For so long I found that very hard. When I would take the scripture seriously, study the Bible carefully and open my life to the Holy Spirit's tug, if I thought I was seeing new light, I would blink, squint, and close my eyes. I was so loyal to the orthodoxy of my origins, and I feared that if I followed new light to a new conclusion, it would make me seem ungrateful for my heritage.

But one day I realized that I could both bless the best of my origins *and* embrace the newest light God might reveal. I realized that real maturity is in neither idolizing our theological origins or in scoffing at them. Real maturity means blessing the best of what is behind us *and* following the light that is before us, giving thanks to God for those who shaped us in the past, *and* being honest with the new light that waits to be followed. We really can bless the best of our origins with one hand and, with the other hand, take hold of new light on God's truth. We don't have to scoff at one to embrace the other.

Every now and then, following Jesus will mean finding a place to stand. But mostly it will mean finding a path to walk, following new light, growing in grace, and being changed more and more into the likeness of our Lord Jesus. But be warned. The path is steep. There is this trouble with the truth: It will make us free, but before it will finally make us free, it will likely make us blink. Amen.

If we are blinded by darkness,
we are also blinded by light.
When too much light falls on everything,
a special terror results.

—Annie Dillard
Pilgrim at Tinker Creek

And [Jesus] said to them, "Therefore every scribe who has
been trained for the kingdom of heaven is like the master of
a household who brings out of his treasure what is new and
what is old."

—Matthew 13:52

THE WEIGHT OF PAIN

Losing feels worse than winning feels good. Lewis Grizzard, the famous twentieth-century American philosopher, left us with many memorable sentences, but none of them ever landed closer to the truth than this one: "Losing feels worse than winning feels good."

I hadn't thought about those words for several years. And then, one Saturday evening, I was sitting out on the front steps, watching the sunset, when a question wandered up, uninvited, and sat down next to me. I don't know from where the question came. We weren't expecting company. But this question I'd never seen before just wandered up and joined me. And now it won't leave me alone. I can't get the question to leave.

The question is, "Why does pain almost always seem to weigh more than joy?" That's the question that found me out on the steps. It's a hard question. (It'll teach you not to sit idly around doorsteps on Saturday evenings.) It is sort of a companion to Lewis Grizzard's old adage. When I met this question, "Why does pain almost always seem to weigh more than joy?" I immediately recalled the old line, "Losing feels worse than winning feels good," which, I think, is just another way of saying that, for many people, the pain of life weighs more than the joy of life.

I wonder why it is that way. Why does pain almost always seem to weigh more, to have more substance, to impact us more powerfully, than joy? For many people, the moments that have been most life-changing have been, not the moments of joy, but the moments of pain. Certainly not for all people is that true, but, for many people, life has been transformed, lifted, and turned toward God more by trouble and pain than by ease and joy. Not in every case, but in many cases, pain does seem to weigh more than joy.

That seems to be what Paul is saying in 2 Corinthians 12:1-10. He says that he has been struggling with some problem that just will not go away. Paul does not identify the exact nature of this lingering problem. Instead, he refers to it by the painful image of "a thorn in the flesh."

Students of scripture have long speculated as to what the thorn in the flesh might have been; a chronic disease, poor eyesight, depression, loneliness . . . who can say? What we do know is that Paul was obviously living with some persistent difficulty, something painful and troubling. He says that he prayed for God to take away the pain, to remove the thorn in his flesh, to deliver him from his struggle. But God's reply to Paul's plea was that Paul would have to live with his painful difficulty. God did not promise Paul deliverance from his pain. Rather, God promised Paul sufficient strength to live with the pain, to bear the pressure, to keep going despite the difficulty.

Not only did God promise Paul sufficient strength to live with his "thorn in the flesh," but God also indicated to Paul that Paul was a better person with his pain than ever he would have been without his pain:

Three times I appealed to the Lord about this [thorn in the flesh], that it would leave me, but [the Lord] said to me, "My grace is sufficient for you, for power is made perfect in weakness." (v. 9a)

Here is a great paradox, an amazing irony, a wonderful mystery: Strength is made more perfect, more complete, in weakness. In other words, God told Paul that Paul was a better person, a more useful person, a more opened-up-to-God person with his painful struggle than ever Paul would have been without it. So Paul then came to a magnificent conclusion:

I will boast all the more gladly of my weaknesses, so that the power of Christ may dwell in me. Therefore I am content with weaknesses, insults, hardships, persecutions, and calamities for the sake of Christ; for whenever I am weak, then I am strong. (v. 9b-10)

Paul did not seek his pain, and, if he could be delivered from it, it would please him, but, since he has it, and since it is apparently a pain that is his for life, he is going to embrace the pain and live fully into it because he has learned that his pain is actually opening him up to God in ways that joy and success never would have.

Paul's words land pretty close to Psalm 119:71, where the Psalmist said, "It is good for me that I have been afflicted" (KJV). Now isn't that something? "It is *good* for me that I have been afflicted." Its a good thing I didn't write Psalm 119:71. If I had been writing that verse, I'd have probably said, "It is bad for me that I have been afflicted." Or, "It is uncomfortable for me that I have been afflicted." Or, it is inconvenient for me, or troublesome for me, or unfair for me, or anything but good for me that I have been afflicted. What in the world was the Hebrew poet thinking when he wrote those words, "It is good for me that I have been afflicted"?

Perhaps the Psalmist was thinking the same thing as Paul. Perhaps the Psalmist had already discovered what Paul would later learn, that somehow our lives are opened up to God by an unbearable weight of pain in ways they never would have been by an unbroken flight of joy. It is true. It is mysterious, strange, indefinable, and inexplicable, but it is nonetheless true that we are made better, deeper, quieter, kinder people by the pain of life's struggles. We do somehow become stronger at the very places at which we are broken. God's presence does somehow seem to enter and change our lives and strengthen and soften and deepen our lives through doors pried open by pain, left open by struggle, and propped open by life's hardest twists and turns.

Now, we have to be careful here. If we aren't careful, we will say too much. There are a couple of bends in this road at which we must slow down and be very careful. For one thing, we must be careful lest we conclude that if God uses life's most painful moments in ways that cause us to become deeper and better people, then we should go out and seek pain and brokenness. But that, of course, is not the case. We need not seek pain. There is plenty of pain in this world. We don't have to go looking for pain. If we just live long enough, pain will come.

This brings us to another bend in the road that beckons us to slow down and be careful. Not only must we be careful lest we conclude that we should seek pain, but we must also be careful lest we conclude that if God uses the pain of life to change us for the better, then God sends to us life's painful problems, tragedies, and calamities in order to change us. At that precarious bend in the road we must slow our words to a crawl, lest we say more than we know.

Some popular theology would say that everything that comes to our lives is sent from God or willed by God. There are some Bible verses one can employ in support of such an idea. But when I read the four Gospels and watch what Jesus does and when I ponder the life of Jesus as the Word of God, I cannot embrace the popular theology that assigns all of life's pain and tragedy to the will of God. I cannot embrace the idea that God sends us calamity to "get our attention" and change us. Jesus gave us our best look yet at who God is, how God acts, and what God does, and Jesus never sent anyone a disease; Jesus only healed diseases. Jesus never caused anyone's death; he only raised people from death. Jesus never sent a calamity to a city; he only wept over the calamity that he knew was bound to come into people's lives. Thus, I find it impossible to embrace the popular theology that many thoughtful Christians embrace, the theology that assigns all this pain to the will of God.

When I read the Scriptures in the light of the life of Jesus, I am left to say, not in a shout of certainty, but at least in a whisper of conviction, that the pain that comes to us in life comes to us, not because God wills it for us, aims it at us, sends it to us, or lays it on us, but because we live in a world where there are germs and diseases, where there is death and loss. We live in a world where there is disappointment and complexity and pain, and if that pain can come to anybody, it can come to everybody. And when it comes, it comes, not because God sent it, but because that is the nature of life in this world. Some of the pain we could avoid by making better choices and different decisions, but most of it comes just because we live in a world where bad things can happen.

But when those bad things happen, when pain rolls over us and life seems unbearable and the heart breaks, it is the nature of God to resurrect from the brokenness something new. That is God's way. That is how God is. I don't believe God sends the pain to make us better, but I do believe that when the pains and losses and struggles come, our lives are somehow opened up to God's presence in new ways, and God then somehow makes us new people—people who are kinder, quieter, more sensitive and discerning, and more able to enter into the pain of those around us.

Our Lord Jesus said that one of these days, the last word is going to be joy, but that between now and then, pain will have a word with us. When the pain comes—and it will—the God we love and trust will be with us and for us, and the God we love and trust will enter the deepest corners of our lives through new doors that pain alone can open. And, by the grace of God at work in our lives, we can be changed, transformed, made better by the pain we endure.

Here is a great wonder: When the worst weight of pain is pressing down the hardest, we are most opened up to the presence of God that deepens our life, softens our eye, lowers our voice, and opens our heart. Here is a great wonder: It is while the awful weight of pain is bearing down on us that God gets God's best chance to lift us to the place where joy always wanted to take us but couldn't. Here is a great wonder: Pain can prop open a door that joy, despite its best efforts, could never quite open.

Ernest Hemingway, in a letter to F. Scott Fitzgerald, once wrote, "When you get the . . . hurt, use it."[7] And Emily Dickinson, in her "letter to the world that never wrote to her," once said, concerning the fact that pain weighs more than joy,

> Essential oils are wrung—
> The Attar from the Rose
> Be not expressed by Suns—alone—
> It is the gift of Screws[8]

Indeed. What soft, sunlit joys cannot coax from us, the hard turning screws of pain can wring from us. Joy always wanted to make us deeper, stronger, softer, and kinder. But for making us deeper, stronger, softer, and kinder, pain carried more weight. Amen.

The world breaks everyone,
and afterward
many are strong at the broken places.
—Ernest Hemingway
A Farewell to Arms

Very truly, I tell you,
you will weep and mourn . . .
you will have pain,
but your pain will turn into joy.
—John 16:20

LIVING IN THE GAP

BETWEEN WHAT WE DREAMED
AND WHAT WE GOT

After all those years of stumbling around in the middle of nowhere, dealing with all the conflict and controversy of his contrary constituency, you'd like to think that Moses would get to lead the parade into the land of promise. But, alas, almost was as close as he came:

> Then Moses went up . . . to the top of Pisgah . . . and the Lord showed him the whole land . . . and the Lord said to Moses, "This is the land I promised to Abraham, to Isaac and to Jacob . . . I have let you see it with your eyes, but you shall not cross over there." (Deut 34:1-4)

Moses could see it, but he could not have it. The land of promise lay just out of Moses' reach, and he died without quite making it to the promised land.

It's an old, old story, covered in dust, tucked away in one of the Old Testament's quieter corners. But somehow you know, as soon as you hear it, that Moses' moment on Mount Pisgah is a parable of real life in the real world for many people today. Moses' life ended on Mount Pisgah, somewhere between what he dreamed and what he got. He came close, so close he could see the promised land. But there was, for Moses, a wide gap between *seeing* his "dream-come-true" and *having* his dream come true. Moses lived and died somewhere between what he dreamed and what he got.

And Moses wasn't the first. The book of Hebrews says there were others, before Moses, who had a similar experience. Abraham, Isaac, and Jacob . . . all died without "receiving the promises." From a distance they saw and greeted the promise, but they never actually received the promises that had been made to them. I think I would rather it said, "Because Abraham, Isaac, and Jacob had faith, all their promises came through, and all their dreams came true." But such was not the case. For Abraham, Isaac, and Jacob, there was a lot of lifelong stumbling around somewhere between what they dreamed and what they got. And they were not the last. After them, there was Moses. And Moses was not the last, either, was he? For many, many people there is this wide space between life as they dreamed it and life as they live it.

Now, of course, we should probably pause here to acknowledge the fact that, for some people, the gap between what they dreamed and what they got is on the high side, the plus side, the bright side. For many people, life has unfolded in ways far more wonderful than their fondest dreams. For some, the gap between what they dreamed and what they got is a gap that leaves them filled with wonder and gratitude for a life that has been much better than they ever dreamed life could be or thought life would be.

But, for many others, the gap is on the other side. For many, many people, life has unfolded in surprisingly hard ways. They have had to bear burdens they never dreamed they would have to bear. For so many people, there is this bewildering, disappointing, exhausting gap between what they dreamed, or assumed, or expected about life and the life they find themselves living. And what then? What do we do when life unfolds in ways we never imagined or expected or dreamed? Does the Bible offer us any help for living in the gap between what we dreamed and what we got?

There is an Old Testament passage that speaks to people for whom life has unfolded in hard ways they never would have dreamed. The passage is Jeremiah 29, which is the letter Jeremiah sent to the people of Judah who had been carried away into exile. They had been uprooted from their homeland, carried away captive to Babylon, torn from the familiar, and thrust into a strange new world. They were hoping to get back home before too long. They were dreaming of a brief exile and a soon return to normal. They even had some preachers who encouraged them in their optimism. But Jeremiah got wind of all this back in Jerusalem, and he fired off a letter to the exiles. In the letter, Jeremiah said, "Don't believe those starry-eyed, utopian sermons about how everything will be alright real soon and you'll be home before you know it. Don't keep dreaming those dreams of a brief exile and a quick return, because it isn't going to happen. In fact," wrote Jeremiah, "you are going to be there in Babylon for seventy years. So, build a house. Plant a garden. If you don't go ahead and live life as fully as you can in Babylon, you will never fully live life anywhere. This exile, this displacement, this situation in which you find yourselves is going to last seventy years."

Can you imagine how that must have felt to the exiles? Think about it . . . Seventy years. Anyone who was old enough to understand the letter was pretty much assured that they were going to live the rest of their lives in what they had thought was a temporary situation. They thought this difficulty would pass, change, go away. They dreamed of life soon getting back to normal. But Jeremiah said, "No. You are up against something that isn't going to change. This is your life."

Jeremiah told his weary, displaced friends to come to terms with life as it was. He did not tell them that if they prayed harder or had more faith, they would be rescued from their tough situation. Rather, he just told them to come to terms with the way their life had unfolded and to live into and through the only life they were going to have—life in Babylon. Jeremiah's medicine was not pleasant. He offered God's children a hard dose of realism. That is a part of how we live in the gap between what we dreamed and what we got—by coming to terms with life as it is.

In church, we sometimes don't do well with coming to terms with life as it is. We sometimes tend to take the noble virtue of optimism and baptize it into a sort of "onward-and-upward-theology" that is more akin to the utopian prophets of a brief exile than it is to Jeremiah's honest proclamation of a lifelong displacement. To be sure, the church does have a gospel of hope to proclaim. But sometimes, every now and then, the church needs to hold hands with Jeremiah and help people come to terms with the truth that some of life's difficulties, complexities, and losses are not going to fade, change, or be repaired.

I have often thought how helpful it might be to people if they could just once hear it said, out loud, on a Sunday, in a church, from a pulpit, that "some dreams just have to be given a decent burial." That, I think, is what Jeremiah was saying to the people in exile: "There are some dreams that just have to be given a decent burial." Sometimes life unfolds in hard ways. We find ourselves living in the gap between what we dreamed and what we got. One of the ways we live in that gap is by coming to terms with the fact that some of life's hardness, disappointment, and complexity is simply not going to change, fade, or go away. There are some dreams that just have to be given a decent burial.

But that is not all there is to say. There is more to say than the vocabulary of realism can pronounce. There is something else—

and Someone else—at work. God is not done or finished or through. For a glimpse of the radical and surprising and wonderful not-yet-visible work of God, listen to these stunning words from the Gospel of Luke: "Blessed are you who weep now, for you will laugh" (6:21). Whatever else this verse means, it must at least mean that, as surely as there are some dreams that don't come true, there is also some truth that doesn't come dreamed. There is some as-yet-unseen work of God that transcends our wildest dreams. It is the truth that doesn't come dreamed, and it will be God's joy to bring it to pass. Perhaps that is what Paul meant when he spoke of realities that "no eye has seen, nor ear heard, nor the human heart conceived, what God has prepared for those who love [God]" (1 Cor 2:9).

To all of God's bruised, weary, disappointed children let us say, not in a certain shout, but in a believing whisper, that there is more to life than the dreams that don't come true. There is also the truth that doesn't come dreamed; the unseen, unheard, unimagined truth of what God has not yet done. Amen.

What might have been and what has been
Point to one end, which is always present.
Footfalls echo in the memory
Down the passage which we did not take
Toward the door we never opened.

—T. S. Eliot
"Burnt Norton"

All of these died in faith without having
received the promises, but from a distance
they saw and greeted them.

—Hebrews 11:13a

WHY DOESN'T GOD DO MORE?

Why doesn't God do more? If God protects some from tragedy, why doesn't God spare everyone? If God intervenes in some dreadful situations, why doesn't God fix every terrible problem? Why doesn't God do more?

"Why doesn't God do more?" is a quiet question that wandered around, homeless and nameless, inside my soul for many years. I had no syllables to wrap around it. Then one day I stumbled over those whispers John saved from the edge of Lazarus' grave: "Could not he who opened the eyes of the blind man have kept this man from dying?" (11:37). Those words are only incidental to the larger story of the raising of Lazarus, but, though they may have started out minor on John's page, they ended up major in my ear.

"Could not he who opened the eyes of the blind have kept this man from dying?" That incidental question climbed out of the Bible and put a roof over the head of a wordless mystery that had long languished inside my soul. It ceased to be the echo of someone else's quiet question about Jesus and became instead a frame around my own quiet question about God. There are few questions in all the world that land nearer to the great mystery of why God's abiding love combined with God's enduring power don't equal God's constant protection, than the one someone whispered at Lazarus' grave. It is in that sense that the quiet question first asked about Jesus has become, for me, a parable of one of life's enormous, unresolvable mysteries: "Why doesn't God do more?" If God is as loving as we've said, and if God is as powerful as we've heard, then why doesn't God do more? If God cares, and if God can, then why doesn't God step in and change more, heal more, fix more, do more?

There are, of course, some familiar answers that are eager to reply to that one quiet question. One answer is that God may have already spared us from many things of which we are not aware. Who of us can know from what terrible problems we have been spared by the gentle providence of God?

It is true: None of us knows from what we have been spared because the things from which we have been spared didn't happen to us. We can't know what they *were* because they *weren't*. (It's sort of like that great line from a sad ballad by the famous twentieth-century American poet, Randy Travis: "Since the phone still ain't ringing, I assume it still ain't you."[9] Since many awful things haven't happened to us, perhaps God has spared us many times.)

Who can know what God has done? Maybe God has been busy doing more than we have noticed. This is a great mystery, and it is one answer to the quiet question, "Why doesn't God do more?" But, of course, that leaves us with all the tragedies from which people are not spared, which leaves us yet to wonder, "Why doesn't God protect all God's children from everything tragic? If God spares some of God's children from some awful things, why doesn't God spare all of God's children from all terrible things?"

Perhaps the most popular answer is that all the terrible things from which God does not spare people are a part of God's plan.

Many wonderful people find comfort in this idea. It imposes a sense of order on the world and defends the sovereignty of God. It buttresses the idea that God is in control of every occurrence. It sounds good, and it has a sort of religious ring to it, but it raises as many questions as it answers. Think of all the violent crimes that destroy lives and break hearts. Think of all the children who live in fear of their own parents. Think of all the families torn asunder by dreadful diseases, relentless addictions, and unbearable problems, not of their own making. Think of Kosovo's tormented refugees. Someday, God's will *will* be done on earth just as it is in heaven—but not now. Now, it is just as William Sloane Coffin said when his son was killed, "Of all hearts, God's heart was most broken."[10]

Of course, the problem is that once we say that everything is not a part of God's will, we open up the prospect that some of life is random. That is a troubling idea to those of us who yearn for a more orderly, cause-and-effect world, but I find it less troubling than the notion that everything that happens is a part of God's plan because that would mean that God was planning things like Hurricane Mitch for Honduran children and drive-by bullets for urban toddlers. I choose to believe that such things are against the will of God and outside the plan of God, though I find that hard to say because I am also certain that there is a gentle providence of God at work in our world. This is a great mystery.

Another answer to the "Why doesn't God do more?" question is, "Well, God does do more for those who pray harder and have more faith." I would like very much for this to be the answer. I want it to be true. And it is true, in the sense that prayer puts us in touch with God's goodness, creativity, comfort, and strength in ways that often cause healing, direction, and resolution to occur in mysterious, mystical, miraculous ways. But the rest of the truth is that sometimes the people who pray the hardest and believe the greatest do not get the miracle. Sometimes we pray and pray and believe and believe, but God still does not do what we hoped. Then what?

Then we have to relearn the fact that prayer is not the leverage we use to convince God to do our will. Prayer is not something we do so we can change God and get God to go along with what we want." Prayer is not the currency we offer God in exchange for getting things to go our way. Prayer is simply the most natural act of life. Everything I fear or dread, everything I love or hope, everything that crushes or bewilders me, I talk to God about because I could not keep myself from talking to God about such things even if I tried. I can no longer think of prayer in terms of whether or not it was answered because prayer is not a transaction that only works if it is answered. If we believe that prayer is a transaction, and that if we can only get it right then we can get God to come around and do our will, then the answer to the question "Why doesn't God do more?" is that God will always do more if we will only pray more. That answer has the authoritative ring of religion to it, and it has a wonderful core of truth in it, but it has been the experience of many people that such a saying is not always entirely true.

Why doesn't God do more? The simplest explanations are to assign all the dreadful, devastating heartaches to the will of God or to blame them on insufficient praying and believing. Those answers impose order on our world, and they help many people cope with life's worst agonies. (And, of course, we can find Bible verses here and there to enlist in support of those ideas, as we can do with many ideas.) But I'm not sure that such answers are true to the best that we know of God. Thus, I cannot completely embrace them, which leaves me without an answer.

I don't have an answer that settles the question, but I do have a confession that I lay down alongside the question. In the face of that one quiet question, "Why doesn't God do more?" my confession of faith is this: "God sometimes does less than we hope, but God always does more than we know." I believe both sides of that confession with equal passion.

Unvarnished honesty requires me to say that God sometimes does less than I hope. I wonder why God doesn't do more, and I don't embrace the idea that it is all because of the will of God or the plan of God or because we didn't pray hard enough or because we didn't have enough faith. In fact, I think that popular version of the faith has actually left many disillusioned with God. There are many people who have given up on God altogether because they were "over-promised." They were taught a version of the faith that left them believing that if they would be good, do right, and have faith, God would protect them from the worst of life's awful tragedies. They expected God to do more. They were holding God to promises God never made, and when life fell apart, God did too, in their minds.

At some point the cycle has to be broken. We cannot go on, generation after generation, reteaching a version of the gospel that implies that if people will pray, serve God, and have faith, they can get God sufficiently in their debt so that God will be obligated to grant them an exemption from the worst that life can bring.[12] As Barbara Brown Taylor has so wisely said, "We must let go of the God who was supposed to be in order to seek the God who is."[13]

God sometimes does less than we hope, and we are left with this unanswerable question, "Why doesn't God do more?" This is half of the truth. The other half of the truth is that God, who sometimes does less than we hope, always does more than we know. In John 11 the one who wondered why Jesus didn't do more did not know what Jesus was about to do. So it is with us.

If clear-eyed realism forces us to say that God sometimes does less than we hope, then wide-eyed faith nudges us to say that God always does more than we know. We never know what God will yet do. And think of this: God has already done for us things we did not know; otherwise we would not have been able to live through the things God did not do. But here we are, alive, having lived through things we would have sworn we could not have endured. But we have lived. We have made it through, by the grace and goodness of the One who is always up to more than we know. All those times when God was doing less than we hoped, God must have been doing more than we knew. Amen.

*Never morning wore to evening,
but some heart did break.*
—Alfred Tennyson
"In Memoriam"

*My God, my God,
why have you forsaken me?
Why are you so far from helping me?
. . . O Lord, do not be far away!*
—Psalm 22:1-2, 19

THE STUMBLING CHILDREN
OF ABRAHAM

Faith is better understood as a verb than as a noun, as a process than as a possession. Faith is more "on-again-off-again"
than it is "once-and-for-all." Faith is not being sure where you
are going, but going anyway.

—Frederick Buechner
Wishful Thinking[14]

Abraham, the great ancestor of our faith, would probably say a
hearty "Amen" to Buechner's description of faith. After all,
for Abraham and Sarah, faith was not a noun for holding on; it
was a verb for moving on. Faith was not something Abraham had
as much as it was something that had Abraham. Instead of saying that Abraham had a lot of faith, we might want to say that
faith had a lot of Abraham. For Abraham, living by faith meant,
as Halford Luccock once wrote, "marching off the map."[15] And
you know that Abraham had to have had his doubts. After all,
remember how Abraham's life of faith unfolded.

All my life I have heard well-intentioned, sincere church-folk
talk about how God honors faith by giving those who obey God
"confirming signs of success." Don't ask Abraham to support
such an idea. Abraham's act of faith did not place his feet on a

smooth pathway paved with confirming signs. Rather, Abraham's faith set his feet to a bumpy trail littered with discouraging problems.

When Abraham's faith nudged him to say, "Yes," when God said, "Go," he encountered one difficulty after another. There was that shameful episode when Abraham resorted to trickery because he imagined that Pharaoh wanted to kill him so he could have Sarah. There was that sad chapter when Abraham, impatient with God, conceived a child with Hagar, which nearly destroyed his marriage to Sarah. There were all those years of longing for a baby to be born. And then, when they finally had a child, Abraham went stumbling up Mount Moriah, knife in one hand, boy in the other, believing that he was going to have to choose between obeying God and being a good father. Such darkness. Such confusion. Such a strange confluence of faith and fear, trust and trouble, hope and darkness. Such was the life of faith for Abraham.

As such, Abraham is perfect for the role in which he is cast by the writer of the book of Hebrews. While we cannot know who wrote Hebrews, it appears to have been a message for late first-century believers who were worn-out, beaten-down, and weary. Tom Long, in his commentary on Hebrews, said this:

> The Preacher sends the sermon we call Hebrews to a congregation he knows. He is not preaching into a vacuum; he is addressing a real and urgent pastoral concern. His congregation is exhausted. They are tired—tired of serving, tired of being whispered about in society, tired of the spiritual struggle. Their hands droop, their knees are weak, and they are losing confidence. Worn down and worn out, they are in danger of dropping their end of the rope and drifting away. Tired of walking the walk, many of them are taking a walk, leaving the community and falling away from the faith.[16]

Why is the community of faith to which the book of Hebrews was written in such a crisis? Why are folks about to give up and fall away? Perhaps they are bewildered by the delay of the return of Christ. Perhaps they have been the victims of persecution. (Both are suggested in the text of the book of Hebrews.) In any case, their confidence is wavering, and their strength is waning. They have many questions and few answers.

Into their darkness comes this sermon we call the book of Hebrews, in which they are encouraged, over and over again, to hold on to their hope and to trust the goodness of God even when they cannot understand the hardness of life. And then, having offered all of those words of encouragement to the congregation, the preacher reminds them that faith, after all, is about trusting even when we cannot see, believing even when we cannot understand, being certain that God will yet have the last word, "despite all the overwhelming, and sometimes devastating, evidence to the contrary."[17]

The writer of Hebrews is not talking about faith as that "sunny-side-of-the-street" optimism that borders on baptized superstition and that is so prevalent in popular theology. Rather, he is talking about faith as trust despite the darkness, faith as believing that it is God's unfailing nature to birth unanticipated goodness out of inexplicable difficulty and unbearable pain. And, of course, his ultimate example of such faith is the faith of Abraham and Sarah—a faith not for those who glide glibly along, claiming absolute certainty and complete clarity, but a faith for those who stumble forward, confessing bewilderment and uncertainty.

Abraham and Sarah, says the writer of Hebrews, were people of faith who went out not knowing where they were going, who stumbled their way through trouble and disappointment, but who never turned back or gave up because they believed there was more to life and more to God than what they could see or feel or explain or prove. They stumbled on, living by faith and finally dying by faith, because, as the writer of Hebrews is bold to say in Hebrews 11:13, "All of these died in faith without having received the promises, but from a distance they saw and greeted them." Now that is real, honest faith. Not faith all dolled up and prettied up and syrupy-sweet. Not faith as a formula for success or a guarantee of answered prayer. No. This is faith for the "dust and blood" of real life: Faith, not as the promise of sufficient magic to live above the pain of life, but faith as the source of sufficient hope to live into the pain of life, to live through the pain of life and to live beyond the pain of life, faith to keep us on our feet, stumbling along with Abraham and Sarah.

The stories of faith in the book of Hebrews are not just ancient encouragement for some long-lost first-century congregation. They offer livable, contemporary encouragement for real life in the real world right now. The book of Hebrews is a powerful corrective for those popular notions about faith that would almost lead us to believe that if we live with fear or anxiety or depression or doubt, we must not be people of faith. Nothing, of course, could be further from the truth. The book of Hebrews shows us faith covered in the dust and blood and sweat and tears of struggle, uncertainty, and unfulfilled dreams. Here is honest faith: Trusting in the goodness of God—not instead of struggling with fear, anxiety, depression and doubt—but trusting in the goodness of God while struggling with fear, anxiety, depression, and doubt.

That is real faith for real life in the real world. If we struggle with anxiety, fear, depression, or doubt, we must not automatically assume that we have "too little faith." For one thing, who of us can measure faith? And for another thing, even if we could measure faith, we couldn't make ourselves have more of it, anymore than we can make ourselves have less of it. We talk about having "more faith" because that is the only way we know to speak of that which is beyond words. But, here, as elsewhere, Alfred Tennyson's notion that our words "conceal as much as they reveal" holds true. Especially is this so when we say familiar things such as, "If only we had more faith, God would answer our prayers." That statement sounds so logical and religious to say, but think for a moment of what it says about prayer and about God. It says that prayer, which is actually the most natural, simple gift God ever gave us, is now a contest for which only God knows the rules. Would God have a predetermined "amount of faith" someone had to have in order for their prayers to be heard, and not reveal what that required amount of faith was? Would God keep us guessing as to the required "amount of faith?" And even if we knew the required minimum amount of faith God demanded, how would we make ourselves have "more faith?" Do you work it up? Have you ever mustered up a mustard seed more of faith? Can you make yourself have *less* faith? Then how could you make yourself have *more*?

I suppose we will always talk the way we always have about having more faith. It has always been that way. Jesus' first friends implored him to increase their faith. And so do we. We always will. After all, there are many Bible verses that seem to measure amounts of faith. But our words conceal as much as they reveal.

How much faith is enough? When we try to measure how much faith we have, an awful lot "breaks through language and escapes." And anyway, perhaps the notion that *we have faith* does not exhaust the whole truth. Maybe the rest of the truth, the biggest part of the truth, is that *faith has us*. Sometimes it almost seems more true to say that faith has us. Faith keeps tugging at us, pulling on us, moving us forward, slowly, slowly, the stumbling children of Abraham. We stumble forward, believing there is more to life than we can see. We stumble forward, believing the goodness of God even when we are up against the hardness of life. We believe more than we don't believe, so we keep trying to do the right thing, trusting that our labors are not in vain.

Faith has us, even when we don't feel that we have faith. Faith keeps us going, keeps us helping and serving and giving. And in our brightest, clearest, most mature and faith-filled moments, we sense that we aren't just futile laborers, breaking rocks in the sun. We sense that we are midwives who are helping God give birth to unanticipated, even unseen, new life and goodness. Such is the life of faith for the stumbling children of Abraham. Amen.

The doubt, like the mosquito,
buzzes around my faith.
—Emily Dickinson

I believe;
help my unbelief!
—Mark 9:24

TO KNOW THE WILL OF GOD

Poor Paul! False starts, failed efforts, foiled plans, well-intentioned missions that were over before they had begun . . . Such is the nature of Paul's life in Acts 16:

> They went through the region of Phrygia and Galatia, having been forbidden by the Holy Spirit to speak the word in Asia. When they came opposite Mysia, they attempted to go into Bythinia, but the Spirit of Jesus did not allow them; so, passing by Mysia, they went down to Troas. (vv. 6-8)

Poor Paul. He has something to say, but he can't quite find a place in which to say it. He really wants to go to Asia, but that doesn't feel right. He starts out for Bythinia, but that doesn't work out. He goes to Troas, not because he chooses to, but because no place he really wants to go is open to him. Poor Paul . . . all dressed up with no place to go, wandering about in a lavender fog of uncertainty, stuck in Troas, when, in the middle of the night, it all comes clear! Paul has a dream. He sees a vision. He hears a voice: "Paul, we need you in Macedonia. Come over to Macedonia and help us." And with that the fog lifts, the dawn breaks, the light shines through, and the sails go up. According to the writer of Acts,

> When [Paul] had seen the vision, we immediately tried to cross
> over to Macedonia, being convinced that God had called us to
> proclaim the good news to them.

Paul has found his place. He now knows exactly where God
wants him to be! In the span of a single paragraph, in the space
of six verses of Scripture, Paul has gone from stumbling around
without a clue about where God wants him to be to sailing forth
without a doubt about where God wants him to go.

Those are two rather severe extremes on the spectrum of
knowing the will of God. When it comes to the will of God, Paul
seems not to have a clue in verses 6-8, but he seems not to have
a doubt in verses 10-12. Where would you fall on that spectrum?
Do you identify more with the Paul who seems not quite sure
about God's will for his life, or do you resonate more with the
Paul who seems absolutely certain about where God wants him
to be and what God wants him to do?

Fred Craddock, in one of his sermons, said that he has
known some people who talk about the will of God with such
absolute certainty that "you would think they had been walking
all around God taking pictures."[18] That kind of clarity has not
characterized my experience with God. My experience with God
has been more akin to what Thomas Merton once said about
knowing God's will:

> My Lord God, I have no idea where I am going. I do not see the
> road ahead of me. I cannot know for certain where it will end
> . . . And the fact that I think I am following your will does not
> mean that I am actually doing so.[19]

To me, the will of God is not a clear and simple reality. I struggle
with how best to speak of the will of God. I imagine that God is
sometimes surprised to hear some of the human choices and
decisions that are assigned to the will of God. We sometimes say,

"God led us to make this choice," or "God told us to make this move," or "We asked God what we should do, and God said for us to do what we've done, and that's why we did it." I have no right, or reason, to doubt the validity of such words. I know that it sometimes happens that way. I have sensed that at times in my own life. It happened that way for Paul when the Macedonian vision told him exactly where to go, and he went.

But having said that, I also sometimes wonder if, when we are facing decisions where the stakes are very high, maybe we sometimes fall back on the language of the will of God as a way of abdicating responsibility for a decision for which we simply can't bear to take responsibility. That way, if things don't work out, we can always say, "Well, we just moved there because the Lord told us to." "I only married her because the Lord told me she was the one." "We only started that business because the Lord led us to." I don't know, but I sometimes wonder if some of the decisions we assign to the will of God are the decisions that are so enormous that we cannot bear the weight of being accountable for them, so we make God accountable for them. I don't know. One thing is for sure: The will of God is much clearer in retrospect than it is in prospect.[20] It is easier to see where God has guided than it is to discern where God is leading.

But despite all these "I don't knows," I do know something for sure about the will of God: I know for absolute certain that the will of God, what God wants for your life and mine, is for us to cast ourselves upon God's grace, trust ourselves to God's love, share ourselves with God's whole wide world, and give ourselves to God's work of lifting, healing, and loving people, no matter who they are or where they are. That is God's will. God's will is for us to be honest, generous, forgiving, and faithful to God's truth. That is God's will for you and for me. Where we do that and how and with whom . . . well, it may be where we happened

to be born and who we happened to meet and what we happened to be gifted at and interested in that determines where
and how. Or it might just be the will of God. I don't know.

Perhaps no one really knows. But we mustn't let what we
don't know about the will of God trouble us too much. If you and
I just live up to what we do know about the will of God, we'll
have all we can tend to for as long as we live. Then, when we die,
if we're still interested, perhaps we can find out what the will of
God always really was by asking the only One who always really
knew. Amen.

The Road goes ever on and on
Down from the door where it began.
Now far ahead the Road has gone,
And I must follow, if I can,
Pursuing it with weary feet,
Until it joins some larger way,
Where many paths and errands meet.
And whither then? I cannot say.

—J. R. R. Tolkein
The Lord of the Rings

Do not be conformed to this world,
but be transformed by the renewing of your minds,
so that you may discern what is the will of God—
what is good and acceptable and perfect.

—Romans 12:2

THE WIDE REACH OF PENTECOST

One of the many wonderful stories that Garrison Keillor tells is his Christmas monologue called "Exiles," in which Keillor describes the exiles who come home each year to Lake Wobegon, just in time to attend the Christmas Eve mass at Our Lady of Perpetual Responsibility Catholic Church. It is their annual routine, from which they expect nothing new or different from one year to the next. But, one Christmas, they got more than they bargained for. This is how Garrison Keillor describes the scene:

> Father Emil was inspired by the sight of all those lapsed Catholics parading into church . . . and he gave them a hard homily, strolling right down into the congregation. "Shame, shame on us for leaving what we were given that was true and good," he said . . . All of them shuddered a little, afraid he might grab them by their Harris-tweed collars and stand them up and ask them questions . . . They came for Christmas, and here was their old priest . . . whacking them around . . . It was so quiet, you could hear them not breathing.[21]

The pilgrims had journeyed home for Christmas, only to be confronted by something more than they had bargained for. This is not at all unlike the crowd that had gathered in Jerusalem to keep the festival of Pentecost. Parthians, Medes, Elamites, Mesopotamians, Mississippians, Cappadocians . . . from everywhere they came, just as their parents and grandparents before them had come. Only this year something happened for which they had not planned. This year the Pentecostal pilgrims to Jerusalem got more than they bargained for. They heard something they had not anticipated. They encountered truth they had not sought. And on top of that, everyone in this multinational crowd got more than they bargained for in their own language:

> When the day of Pentecost had come, they were all together in one place. And suddenly from heaven there came a sound like the rush of a violent wind . . . Divided tongues, as of fire, appeared among them, and a tongue rested on each of them. All of them were filled with the Holy Spirit and began to speak in other languages, as the Spirit gave them ability. Now there were devout Jews from every nation under heaven living in Jerusalem. . . . Amazed and astonished, they asked, . . . "How is it that we hear, each of us, in our own native language? . . . All were amazed and perplexed, saying to one another, "What does this mean?" (Acts 2:1-5, 7, 12)

The crowds that had converged for the festival of Pentecost were astonished. This multilingual proclamation of God's good story was more than they had bargained for. Thus, "all were amazed and perplexed, saying to one another, 'What does this mean?' " That was the Pentecost question. This was Peter's answer: "I can tell you what this means," he said. "This is the moment of which the prophet Joel was speaking when he said:

> In the last days it will be, God declares, that I will pour out my Spirit upon all flesh, and your sons and your daughters shall prophesy . . . Even upon slaves, both men and women, in those days I will pour out my Spirit; and they shall prophesy. (vv. 17-18)

That was Peter's answer to the first question of Pentecost, "What does this mean?" But what does Peter's answer mean for our world, here and now? Peter's answer means that God pours out God's Spirit freely and fully without regard for gender, nation, or class. The book of Acts is no friend to doctrines of exclusion and discrimination. It is about a Spirit of God that leaps barriers, crosses borders, defies categories, and removes walls. The presence of Jerusalem's enormous, multicultural, multiethnic, multilingual crowd was just the right setting for God's Spirit to come down in a new way. It serves as a powerful symbol of the universal embrace of the Spirit of God, the Spirit that favors no nation or race or class or gender over any other.

There is a familiar poem, "Mending Wall" by Robert Frost, in which the poet writes, "Something there is that does not love a wall, that wants it down." According to the book of Acts, the Holy Spirit, the Spirit of God, will not abide or obey a wall. The Spirit of God will leap a wall, deny a wall, defy a wall, undo a wall. The Holy Spirit does not love a wall. The embrace of the Spirit is as wide as the world—no boundaries, no barriers, no walls, no favorites.

The wide reach of Pentecost reminds us that God has no favorite nation. When I worked in Washington, D.C., I used to drive a few blocks out of my way so that I could see the Washington Monument, ringed by the beautiful circle of United States flags. It was a moving sight, of which I never grew tired. But I also knew that, even if you took all those United States flags and sewed them together into one huge flag, it still would not be large enough to wrap around the tiniest Bible. We do not have a national faith, a national gospel, or a national God. We have a global gospel that knows no favorite nation. That is the message of Pentecost in particular and of the book of Acts throughout.

To be filled with the Spirit is to know intuitively that God not only has no favorite nation, but that God also has no favorite race or gender. In the years of my childhood most churches in my part of the world had among their most frequently sung songs the old hymn "Pentecostal Power":

> Lord, as of old at Pentecost
> Thou didst thy power display,
> With cleansing purifying flame
> Descend on us today.

After singing that first verse, we would all join in on the chorus, "Lord, send the old time power, the Pentecostal power." I remember it well, though it has been many years. I remember singing it gladly, joyfully, and enthusiastically. I also remember that in some of those churches there were times when ushers kept an eye on the door to make sure that no African-American people came in. And if anyone's *daughter* had come forward to say that God was calling her to preach, she might have been sent back to her pew as mistaken. And yet, we sang for the Pentecostal power to fall, never guessing that our deeds contradicted the wide-open embrace that the Pentecost of Acts chapter two celebrates, demands, gives, and requires. If the Pentecostal power for which we sang had indeed "fallen on us," I suspect that—to borrow a phrase from Annie Dillard—it might have blown us to smithereens.[22]

When we are filled with the Holy Ghost, when we are truly Pentecostal, then we only want to be in on what God is up to. And what God is up to has a wide embrace and does not love a wall. Amen.

How often, in the church, do we try to say where the Spirit may or may not blow, when the only thing God has asked us to do is to try and keep up with it wherever it goes?

—Barbara Brown Taylor
Bread of Angels

Then Peter began to speak to them: "I truly understand that God shows no partiality, but in every nation anyone who fears [God] and does what is right is acceptable to [God].

—Acts 10:34-35

THE THEOLOGY OF EXTREMITY

What matters most to God? In recent years that question has grown larger and deeper at the center of my soul. My struggle to discern what really matters most to God has settled around a rather unsettling phrase: "the theology of extremity." It is a phrase that came to me one day while I was visiting in a home where there was no food for the rest of the month. As I sat with the family, on one level I listened to them and made notes about their situation and how our church might be helpful. But on another level, simultaneously, I found myself thinking back through my day. It just happened that on that very day I had spent a good portion of the morning worrying over something I can't even remember now, except that it was some peripheral liturgical question. As I sat there in that home, I found myself judged by the amount of interest and energy I had devoted to something that mattered much to me, but that did not, as the old colloquialism goes, "amount to a hill of beans" when laid alongside the question of whether or not a family was going to have groceries before the first of the month. (In fact, despite my love for and commitment to the liturgical way of worship, I would have to say that in the face of that family's need, an actual hill of real beans would have amounted to much more than the matter that had so consumed me.)

As I walked away from that house, I was struck by the phrase, "the theology of extremity." I thought to myself, "Our practical theology, our everyday way of thinking about God and life, must somehow be colored by the extremity in which God's children live because that is what matters most to God." I had that thought, or it had me. And then, I sort of buried it.

But it staged an Easter on me about eight months later. I was walking the dusty lanes of a small village in the hills of Honduras when that phrase I had buried in West Jackson ambushed me in Central America. I was judged by a question that would not let me be: Alongside the enormous needs of the poorest of God's children, how much do many of the matters that we call important really matter? You don't have to be a Bible scholar to know that human extremity matters to God infinitely more than much of what matters to most of us. By the light of the blazing Honduran sun, in the faces of very poor children, I thought I saw a glimpse of what matters most to God, and I heard again, from somewhere far beyond, or somewhere deep inside, that phrase I had heard once and buried alive, "the theology of extremity." It was a moment not unlike what our Quaker friends call "an opening," and it opened my life in a new way to those old words the prophet Micah said, "Here is what God requires: Do justice . . . Love kindness . . . Walk humbly." Those words are stark, barren, demanding and extreme in their purity and simplicity. Micah said, "You think that what matters most to God is your burnt offerings, your rituals of sacrifice, your religious exercises and ceremony. But that is not what matters most to God. What God wants, what God requires, what matters most to God is that you do justice and love kindness and walk humbly."

In the New Testament, James says it another way: "Religion that is pure and undefiled before God, the Father, is this: to care for orphans and widows in their distress, and to keep oneself unstained by the world" (Jas 1:27). And Jesus says it still another way:

> Then the king will say to those at his right hand, "Come, you that are blessed by my Father, inherit the kingdom prepared for you from the foundation of the world; for I was hungry and you gave me food, I was thirsty and you gave me something to drink, I was a stranger and you welcomed me, I was naked and you gave me clothing, I was sick and you took care of me, I was in prison and you visited me." (Matt 25:34-35)

It is that basic, according to Jesus. This takes us back to Micah. If we do justice and love kindness, we will inevitably give ourselves, in some fashion or other, to the hungry, the thirsty, the stranger, the sick, the poor, the shackled. And when we do those things, we will be doing what James called "true religion." We will be valuing most what Micah said God values most.

But how might we actually begin to live that way? How might we begin to arrange our values in the light of what matters most to God and establish priorities in the shadow of something like a theology of extremity? Well, perhaps it all begins at the place where Micah's grand verse ends. It just might be that, if we reverse the order of Micah's list, we have one of the ways our life with God actually proceeds.

Micah said there are three things God requires of us, three things that really matter to God: to do justice, to love kindness, and to walk humbly with God. If we take that trio and line them up in reverse order, here is what we have: Walk humbly with God, love kindness, and do justice. Perhaps it is in that order that those three realities unfold. We begin by walking humbly with God, by leading a life of quiet prayer to God, silent centering on

God, and open listening for God. It is in that devotional side of life that we begin to walk humbly with God.

When we walk humbly with God, we are changed. Because our lives are punctuated by daily times of silence and prayer, they become colored by a quiet spirit of devotion. We speak less often and less loudly. We become more sensitive to others because we are walking humbly with our God. Then eventually, out of the depths of walking humbly with God, we simply discover one day, perhaps to our great surprise, that more than anything else, we love kindness. And once we come to love kindness, we then have to do justice. I say we "have to" because we can't keep ourselves from it. Our great passion in life becomes doing justice for the weak and poor. We seek out those who are living on the hard edge of life, not because we think we ought to, but because we couldn't keep ourselves from doing justice on behalf of the powerless even if we tried.

Perhaps that is how our life with God grows deeper and wider. We walk humbly with God in prayer, silence, and devotion. Then, out of that new depth, we develop a wider eye of compassion. We begin to love kindness, to value steadfast loving kindness above all other things. We invest our lives, our time, our money, our energy, and our influence in bringing justice to those who are most in need of loving kindness, steadfast mercy, and a just world in which to live. And then we are doing, according to Micah, James, and Jesus, the sort of things that matter most to God.

Of course, it's not that simple. After all, there are many things in life that matter. And yet . . . the truth is, we do fret too much over too many things that matter too little. If we stare into the face of enough pain, if we get close enough to extreme human need, it will force us to rethink a lot of what we think matters. The theology of extremity will leave us with less interest in "much ado about nothing," and it will fill us with new passion for what matters most to God. The theology of extremity will transform us in a deep and indefinable way because, once we begin to live in the light of the shadow of the world's extremity, it is hard ever to see things the same as before.

The theology of extremity has a mysterious mystical side and a simple practical side. The mystical side of the theology of extremity grows, in part, out of our sense of connectedness to all the people of the world. Think about it: Somewhere in the world, in every moment of every day, one of God's children is in dreadful extremity. Thus, how do we justify the energy we invest in peripheral issues while any one of God's children is starving or freezing or dying or weeping? As long as anyone in the world is in extremity, how can sensitive believers be consumed with pettiness? Think of it this way: If someone we love more than life itself were to die a tragic death, how would we act in our grief? Perhaps we would speak softly, ponder the great realities of life, and turn aside from the senseless pursuit of trivial fussiness. We would go deep into our soul and deep into God. We would renew our focus on the things that matter most. Now, consider the fact that every day, somewhere in the world, one of God's children is experiencing the tragic death of someone they love more than life itself. Someone somewhere is always in that kind of awful extremity. As children of the God who is love, shouldn't we be conscious, in the depth of our soul, of the extreme pain that is present in someone somewhere all the time? Since we are always living in the shadow of someone's extreme pain, shouldn't we be perpetually living in the light of the theology of extremity, caring deeply and praying without ceasing for extremities unseen to us but somehow not unknown?

The mystical side of the theology of extremity is shaped, in part, by our sense of connectedness to others, but it also emerges whenever we honestly embrace the certainty of our own ultimate moment of extremity, the moment of our own death. If we lived each day of our lives in the light of the certainty of our own death, we would often say to ourselves: "Why am I fretting so over this worry or that frustration? On the day I die, is this going to matter? If I were on my death bed, would I be irritated by this or angry at that?" To live as though someday will be the last day is another way to begin to embrace the clarity that the theology of extremity brings to life.

This is the mystical side of the theology of extremity: living in the shadow of the world's pain, living in the light of our own death, living as though everyone who suffers is someone we know, and living each day as though some day is going to be the last day. To begin to think this way is to begin to embrace the theology of extremity in a quiet, deep, mystical way. This is dangerous, of course. Overly embraced, the theology of extremity will do us in. We cannot bear the burdens of the world, and we cannot live each day as though it will be the last. Such intensity we were not made to endure. Embraced to extremes, the theology of extremity would become baptized co-dependence. It would not be a healthy way to live. Rightly embraced, however, the theology of extremity will color our lives without consuming them.

This brings us to the simple, practical side of the theology of extremity. Once the mystical side of the theology of extremity begins to ferment in our souls, it has a very practical result: We speak differently. Specifically, we speak differently when we react to life's frustrations, disappointments, inconveniences, and problems. If I live each day with a quiet awareness of the deep sadness, terrible hunger, and unbearable pain that is always someone's somewhere, then how can I lose my temper and speak unkindly in the face of lost laundry, late planes, or long lines? If I live each day in the light of my own death, how can I say angry words over a dented fender or spilled milk?

In a world full of starving, dying, hurting people, I cannot speak arrogantly about my little inconveniences if I am awake to the enormous extremity of others. To embrace rightly the deep, mystical side of the theology of extremity is to find ourselves with a new, simple, very practical phrase often on our lips: "If this is the worst thing that ever happens to us, we will have had a wonderful life." When we embrace the theology of extremity, we can find a thousand occasions to say that phrase instead of speaking unkindly or angrily. Indeed, to look honestly at life through the lens of the theology of extremity is to sometimes chuckle at things over which we once would have growled. Why? Because the theology of extremity has become our new measure of what matters.

This brings us back to Micah's short list of the things that matter most. Of course, it isn't as simple as Micah's short list. There are many things that matter much: relationships, friendships, the new bike, the mountain hike, the play, the song, the anniversary, the birthday, the family around the table, the visit to the nursing home, the wedding, the vacation, the education, the graduation, the walk, the art, the ethics, the baptism, the Bar Mitzvah, the call, the card, the note. The list is long of all the things that we know in our souls really do matter. In a sense, everything matters. In another sense, too many things get much too much of our attention, while life's great issues lie untended. And sometimes, what really matters is the tiny, human, ordinary thing—not the big, impressive, religious thing. We must learn to care about the right thing at the right moment. We must somehow develop a pure eye, an eye for what matters most to God, for what matters most to the people we love, for what matters most to those we have never met or seen. The theology of extremity helps us to see, with a clearer eye, the things that matter most.

According to Micah, what matters most to God is that we walk humbly, love kindness, and do justice. We actually think there has to be more, that there must surely be something more to our lives with God than just that. But if we gave ourselves to those things that matter most to God, it is likely that we would find just the basics to be quite enough, more than enough. In a world of severe extremity, just doing the basics would be all we could embrace and then some. What if we discover one day that, all along, that was what really mattered most to God? Amen.

Once you learn how to die,
you learn how to live . . .
When you realize you are going to die,
you see everything much differently.

—Morrie Schwartz
Tuesdays with Morrie

Woe to you . . . for you tithe mint, dill, and cummin, and
have neglected the weightier matters of the law: justice and
mercy and faith. It is these you ought to have practiced
without neglecting the others . . . You strain out a gnat but
swallow a camel!

—Matthew 23:23-24

LIVING IN THE GAP
BETWEEN THE SACRED
AND THE ORDINARY

M any years ago on a cold January morning I was flipping
through the television channels when I stumbled across a
broadcast sponsored by the Catholic diocese of Chicago. It was
called "Mass for Shut-ins." As the program began, the priest said,
"Welcome to Mass for Shut-ins on the second Sunday in Ordinary
Time." If the priest's greeting was designed to corral potential
viewers out there in T.V. land, it certainly worked on me. The idea
of Mass for shut-ins was rather intriguing, but it was that other
phrase that really captured me: "The second Sunday in Ordinary
Time." What I later learned was that, in the priest's mouth, the
words "ordinary" and "time" were spelled with a capital O and a
capital T. They referred to a portion of the liturgical year, a stretch
of weeks called "Ordinary Time."

There is something alluring about that simple phrase,
"ordinary time." Though it occupies a rather minor place on the
calendar of the Christian year, the phrase "ordinary time" feels
large when it falls across our ears. After all, that is where most of
us live most of life, in "ordinary time." Life is punctuated by a
few special moments and grand events—a festival here, a
celebration there—but most of life is lived in ordinary time.

One of the surest signs that we are growing toward a mature, sensitive, open-eyed faith is when we begin to see, more and more frequently and clearly, the sacred presence of God in the most ordinary moments of life. It is a sure sign of deepening faith when we come to see that the gap between the sacred and the ordinary is mostly imaginary—a gap not of God's making, but of ours. When we begin to look at all of life with a sensitive and discerning eye, then the gap between the sacred and the ordinary begins to disappear.

If ever anyone saw a sacred sight in ordinary time, it was Moses. Moses stumbled over God in the most ordinary kind of time. He was at work, doing his job, tending a flock of sheep. It was quite ordinary work, which Moses did in the ordinary way, ordinary day after ordinary day. In the midst of his own ordinary time, though, something surprising caught Moses' eye. He saw a bush burning, but not burning up. He saw enough to make him look again. And the second glance led to a closer look, which in turn led to a life-transforming moment in which Moses found himself on holy ground, in the presence of God. It was, for Moses, an encounter with the sacred in the midst of ordinary time.

Moses' moment serves well as a parable of the truth that God is present in the most ordinary of life's moments and places and deeds. But unless we have an eye out for the sacred in the ordinary, we will miss it. I wonder how much we have missed because we have not learned to see the sacred in life's ordinary moments. That is the truth to which Elizabeth Barrett Browning pointed with her unforgettable verse:

> Earth's crammed with heaven,
> And every common bush is afire with God.
> But only he who sees takes off his shoes,
> The rest sit 'round it and pluck blackberries.[23]

We do not have to miss so much. There is a whole other way to live. It is what the Quaker Thomas Kelly called "life lived on two levels": going about the ordinary, routine tasks of the day, while, at a deeper level, simultaneously seeing the sacred in the most ordinary kind of moment. I fear that I have missed the sacred much more often than I have seen it. But by God's grace, I have recognized some very ordinary bushes ablaze with the light of God's presence.

Once was on an early spring day when Marcia, Joshua, Maria, and I had made a sad journey to help bury one of our dearest friends, a brilliant young husband and father who died far too soon. After the funeral the church hosted a dinner in the fellowship hall. At some point during the meal, I looked across the room at a table full of kids who ranged in age from about eight to fourteen. They had finished eating and had begun to conduct a very sophisticated scientific experiment. They were trying to see what would happen if they put approximately forty-seven packs of Sweet-and-Low into a single glass of tea.

As I watched them hovering over the glass, giggling uncontrollably, stirring their concoction, the rest of the room and all its people disappeared. It was a mystical moment of clarified vision. And something that was both far beyond me and deep within me said, "Look at that wonderful life in the face of death. See that beautiful joy despite this awful pain. Look at those eyes that can dance and weep in the same day, the same hour, the same moment. That table is the Table of the Lord." Now, on one level, anybody could see that it was just a bunch of kids wasting the church's Nutra-Sweet. But on another level, if you had an eye to see it, it was a heart-stopping convergence of the sacred and the ordinary. The centerpiece on the table was a bush burning, if you had an eye that could see such a thing.

There is no more powerful commentary on all of this than those piercing words from the final act of Thornton Wilder's play *Our Town*. His wonderful character, Emily, has died at the age of twenty-six. She is allowed to choose one day of her life to "relive." She chooses her twelfth birthday. Thornton Wilder lets us see the day as Emily relives it, and he allows us to hear Emily's response to it all from the perspective of one who has died and now realizes how precious and sacred is a routine day of ordinary life. As Emily watches her twelfth birthday unfold, she sees everyone rushing about, consumed with this issue or that matter, and she says from her new perspective of death, "I never realized before how in the dark live persons are . . . From morning to night that's all they are— troubled." Though no one can hear her, she pleads with her mother, "Oh, Mama, just look at me one minute as though you really saw me. Let's look at one another." Finally she says, "I can't look at everything hard enough. . . . I didn't realize. So all that was going on and we never noticed . . . Do any human beings ever realize life while they live it, minute by minute? . . . That's all human beings are, just blind people."[24]

Don't you ever wonder how much we have missed? I wonder. I wonder how much of the sacred has slipped past me—unseen, unrecognized, unnoticed. Viktor Frankl once wrote, "Project yourself onto your own deathbed. Now, from that vantage point, what do you wish you had done with your life?"[25] I know what I wish. I wish I had looked harder, with a wider eye and a more sensitive soul, because I suspect I have missed a lot I should have seen. When I project myself onto my own deathbed, that is a part of what I wish. I wish I had looked harder and seen better.

But we are not yet on our deathbed. We are yet alive. So it must not be too late for us to look and see. I am haunted by Emily's plea, "Just look at me one minute as though you really saw me," and by her question, "Do any human beings ever realize life while they live it, minute by minute?" We must learn to see. We must learn from our Quaker friends to stop, to be still, to center down, to be silent enough to hear the sacred and open enough to see the sacred in life's ordinary sounds and sights. We must learn to live into life's sacred ordinary moments. We must learn to look around the table and wonder if this time might be the last time. We may never learn to look at everything hard enough. But we must begin.

We must begin now. Who knows how much of the sacred we have already missed? And who knows how little of life is left? Amen.

I didn't realize.
So all that was going on and we never noticed it . . .
Oh earth, you're too wonderful for anybody to realize you . . .
Do any human beings ever realize life while they live it?
—every, every minute?
—Thornton Wilder
Our Town, Act III

Then Moses said, "I must turn aside and look at this great sight, and see why the bush is not burned up."

When the Lord saw that Moses had turned aside to see, God called to him out of the bush, "Moses, Moses!"

And he said, "Here I am."

Then [God] said, "Come no closer! Remove the sandals from your feet, for the place on which you are standing is holy ground."
—Exodus 3:3-5

SINNERS IN THE HANDS
OF AN ACHING GOD

I suppose it would be safe to say that, of all the millions of sermons that have ever been preached, none has been more widely read or well known than Jonathan Edwards' famous eighteenth-century exhortation, "Sinners in the Hands of an Angry God." With apologies to Jonathan Edwards, I sometimes wonder if we are sinners in the hands of an *aching* God. I know there are some places in Scripture that suggest we are sinners in the hands of an angry God, but there are also a few passages that cause me to believe we are sinners in the hands of an aching God.

In Luke 13 Jesus was on his way to Jerusalem, on his way to meet persons who would reject his message and refuse God's good news. As he thought of those people, Jesus pronounced over them words, not of anger, but of pain. Jesus did not curse at them; he lamented over them. Jesus did not sound offended by them; he sounded sorry for them: "Jerusalem, Jerusalem, the city that kills the prophets and stones those who are sent to it! How often have I desired to gather your children together as a hen gathers her brood under her wings, and you were not willing" (Luke 13:34). I do not hear in those words an angry Jesus. Rather, I hear an aching Jesus. This is not to say Jesus had no anger. To be sure, Jesus could be quite angry. But on that day, at that place, it was not anger that Jesus' words carried in their hands. It was a quiet, heavy ache, an ache across which we will stumble again when Jesus will gaze out over Jerusalem and say in tearful agony, "If you, even you, had only recognized on this day the things that make for peace! But now they are hidden from your eyes" (Luke 19:42). There is no anger in that voice—only ache.

Now if, indeed, the life of Jesus is the best look we have ever had at who God really is, then what do these glimpses of Jesus suggest to us about God? What does Jesus' agony over people's worst choices tell us about God? I believe that Jesus' agony is the echo of God's ache. After all, we already know that God has this ache. We already know that God aches at the sight of people using their free will to make sinful, dreadful choices that bring hurt and chaos to their lives. We already know about God's ache because of what we learned long ago in Hosea 11. That's the chapter in which God, through Hosea, describes the ingratitude, rebellion, and stubbornness of God's children. God says, "Despite the fact that I have loved them and called to them and cared for them, they have turned away from me." Then God asks, "What am I going to do with people who refuse my call and reject my love?" After which, God answers, "How can I give you up? My heart recoils within me. My compassion grows warm and tender. I will not destroy you, for I am God and not a human. I will not execute my fierce anger."

Here is the aching God. God is angry, but it isn't God's raging anger that carries the day and rules the moment. It is, instead, God's aching love. God says, "My heart is turning over inside me." God's heart recoils at the dreadful sin of God's children, and then God's heart recoils even more at the thought of casting them away. In Hosea 11 God's loving ache runs deeper than God's righteous anger. Having seen that aching side of God, it is no surprise to see Jesus aching at the sight of those who have refused his gifts and rejected his message. After all, Jesus is the way God is, and Hosea told us long ago that God aches at the sight of those who miss so much and lose so much as a result of their refusal of God's love and as a consequence of their rejection of God's way.

I do not mean to suggest there is no anger in God. But when you read the whole Bible and keep an eye out for the whole picture, you can actually begin to ponder the notion that what we call the wrath of God is as much God's ache as it is God's anger. Indeed, when we get to the cross, we see no anger—only pain, agony, ache. That makes me wonder if, when all the truth is known, it will turn out that God's wrath is as much God's ache for us as it is God's anger at us. I don't know, but I suspect that may be so.

We have a tendency to create God in our image and project onto God our capacity to be offended and our need to balance the scales. But if we really believe that the fundamental reality of all of life is the enduring love of God, then we have to let that inform even our view of the wrath of God. I believe at the deep-down core of my being that God's response to our sin, what we call "God's wrath," is more God's loving ache than it is God's offended anger. (Of course, when we speak of God as "angry" or "aching," we must be careful, lest we "anthropomorphize" God; make God into an angry or aching human. We speak of God in these human categories, anger and ache, because we know no other dialect of description. But we must be careful, lest we reshape God into human form. That is why I try to avoid using pronouns for God. God is neither "he" nor "she." Those are human categories, and God is not human; God is God.)

There is a verse in the book of Hebrews that sounds the poignant warning: "It is a fearful thing to fall into the hands of the living God" (10:31). D. H. Lawrence once wrote a poem about that verse. It is called "The Hands of God," and in it the poet says a stunning thing:

> It is a fearful thing to fall into the hands of the living God.
> But it is a much more fearful thing to fall out of them.[26]

The poet was right. The only thing more fearful than falling into the hands of the living God would be to fall out of the hands of the living God. That is the one thing that cannot, does not, will not happen. "Nothing in all creation will be able to separate us from the love of God in Christ Jesus our Lord." God has a hold of us, even when we don't feel that we have a hold of God.[27] We are held in God's hands. We are sinners in the hands of an aching God; a loving, embracing God who has a hold of us and a hold on us for good and forever. Amen.

God is not only the God of the sufferers,
    but the God who suffers.
The pain and fallenness of humanity
    have entered into [God's] heart.
Through the prism of my tears
    I have seen a suffering God.
              —Nicholas Wolterstorff
                Lament for a Son

For I am convinced that neither death,
    nor life,
nor angels,
    nor rulers,
nor things present,
    nor things to come,
nor powers,
    nor height,
nor depth,
    nor anything else in all creation,
will be able to separate us
    from the love of God in Christ Jesus our Lord.
              —Romans 8:38-39

LET THOSE ANGELS BREATHE

Somewhere along the way C. S. Lewis wrote, "There are times in all of our lives when the angels in heaven hold their breath to see which way we will go."[28] It is a beautiful sentence, and though it does not sound to me like a fact, it does, in some mystical, mythical way, ring true, this notion that there are times in all of our lives when the angels in heaven lean out over the balcony and hold their breath to see which way we will go. If there are such moments, I imagine that Mary's moment was one of them: "Will she or won't she? Will Mary obey her deep impulse of love and gratitude? Will she actually rise from her chair and splash the expensive perfume on Jesus? Will she do her simple, careless, lavish act of kindness? Or will she—in the name of pragmatism, good sense, and conventional wisdom—keep her seat, swallow her impulse, and ask someone to pass the potato salad? Will she or won't she?"

If, by some chance, there really are moments when the angels hold their breath to see which way we will go, then maybe Mary's moment was one of them. After all, Mary could have gone the other way. And, had we been in her place, we might have. We might have second-guessed the impulse, swallowed the desire, and stifled the urge to show our gratitude and affection in such a simple, lovely, recklessly lavish way. After all, the perfume was, apparently, quite expensive. It was a gift so lavish that the potential for embarrassment and misinterpretation was quite real. Most of us might have gone the other way at that moment. We might have swallowed that tender impulse. But not Mary. Mary did not sit on her hands. She rose to her feet. She obeyed her highest impulse, did her simple deed, and gave her lovely gift.

And, sure enough, just as we might expect, there was a nearby critic quick to question her sanity, indict her deed, and assail her liberal spirit: "And Judas Iscariot said, 'Why was this perfume not sold for three hundred denarii and the money given to the poor?' " (John 12:5). Now the writer of the Gospel is quick to remind us that we mustn't be taken in by Judas' sudden burst of philanthropic concern. But when we read that parenthetical judgment in John 12:6, we have to remember that this Gospel was not written down until about sixty years after the moment itself. At the moment, there was no commentator offering a carefully reasoned analysis of Judas' ulterior motives. Rather, all we have is Mary, pouring her bottle of perfume on Jesus and letting her hair down to wipe the dust from Jesus' feet. Into that awkwardly beautiful moment Judas goes blundering with his calculator: "Why this waste? Why not sell the perfume and give the proceeds to the poor?" And Jesus looks up at Judas and says, "Leave her alone. She bought it so that she might keep it for the day of my burial. You always have the poor with you, but you do not always have me" (vv. 7-8).

It is a strange little corner of the New Testament, isn't it? For one thing, as much as we might hate to admit it, Judas does seem to have a point. The perfume that formed a puddle beneath the table could have framed a roof over someone's head. The cologne that scattered fragrance around the room could have put food in someone's belly. That is a part of the strain of this passage. Judas, his impure motives notwithstanding, does have a point. And the strain of reading this passage only grows greater with Jesus' response to Judas' complaint: "You always have the poor with you, but you do not always have me." Across the centuries, some have invoked those words to excuse themselves from working, giving, and spending to eradicate poverty and help the poor. "Well, after all, Jesus himself said the poor would always be with us." For shame. To invoke any word of Jesus in defense of a clenched fist and a closed eye and a tight pocket is to deny the very spirit of our Lord.

We cannot read the rest of the four Gospels and press these words of Jesus into the service of a cool nonchalance toward those who are hungry, homeless, cold, and poor. And anyway, the matter becomes much clearer when we discover from where Jesus got the phrase, "You always have the poor with you." Apparently Jesus was not free-lancing when he said those words. It appears that he was quoting from the Hebrew Scriptures. A similar phrase is found in Deuteronomy 15:

> . . . do not be hard-hearted or tight-fisted toward your needy neighbor. You should rather open your hand . . . Give liberally and be ungrudging when you do so . . . Since there will never cease to be some in need on the earth, I therefore command you, "Open your hand to the poor and needy neighbor in your land." (vv. 7, 10, 11)

The phrase, "You always have the poor with you," was not an excuse to avoid involvement in charitable causes. To the contrary, it was a reminder of our perpetual responsibility to help the poor. When Jesus said: "You always have the poor with you," he was quoting from an Old Testament passage: "Since the poor will always be with you, you must always love the poor, give to the poor, care for the poor." But apparently, according to Jesus, in this moment, Mary's act of lavish, reckless, uncalculating love was the right thing for her to do.

What does that mean? I am not sure. But I believe it might mean something like this: It is *always* the right thing to buy bread and milk for the hungry. Sometimes it is the right thing to send someone flowers. It is *always* the right thing to help build a Habitat for Humanity house. Sometimes it is the right thing to paint a picture. It is *always* the right thing to help someone who is in need with rent and medical bills and clothing. Sometimes it is the right thing to sing a song. Jesus seems to be saying that it is *always* right to respond to the poor. But there are also times when it is right and good to lose ourselves in a lavish, reckless, costly act of love and devotion that is beautiful, for no practical purpose, but only for the reason of love. Perhaps that is a part of the truth that hides beneath the dinner table in Bethany. The message seems to be this: "Obey your highest impulses. Release the simple act of kindness and devotion that begs inside your soul to get out." On all days, always, for as long as we live, that will mean caring for God's poor ones. But on some days, in some moments and times, it will mean giving to God, or someone else, a gift of love as impractical as fragrance on the foot.

And apparently, when we do that, when we obey those impulses, when we do the right thing, we never know just how fine the deed is or how far the deed goes. Mary didn't know. When Jesus said, "She has done this to anoint my body for burial," Mary was probably as surprised as anyone in the house. There is nothing in the Scripture to suggest that Mary knew Jesus was about to die. Jesus had raised Mary's brother, Lazarus, from death, so Mary had a heart full of grateful love for Jesus. She wanted to show her love for him, and pouring that perfume on him was the only way she knew. But then Jesus reinterpreted her deed and lifted her simple act to a higher place than Mary ever would have dreamed. Jesus said, "She bought it so that she might keep it for the day of my burial."

Isn't that something? Mary did more than she knew, which seems to be a lesson about the way life is. Whenever we obey our best impulses, say our kindest words, and give our dearest gifts, we never know how far the simple act reaches. Like Mary, there is always something we never know. When we obey our deepest impulses to say the kind word, give the simple gift, or mail the tender note, we think we know what we're doing—and we do know. But we don't really know. Like Mary, we never guess the full beauty and the final significance of our simplest, best gifts of love and care.

You and I can never know the full significance of our kindest words and best deeds. But this much we can know: When, like Mary, we actually go ahead and obey those dearest, deepest impulses and give the helpful gift or write the kind note or say the encouraging word, lives are lifted and blessed and colored for good. And if there really are angels in the balcony, "waiting to exhale," they can at last breathe easy! Amen.

Could mortal lip divine
The undeveloped freight
Of a delivered syllable
'Twould crumble with the weight.
—Emily Dickinson

Do not withhold good . . .
when it is in your power to do it . . .
Do not say . . . "tomorrow I will give it"—
when you have it with you.
—Proverbs 3:27-28

JESUS AND GOD—
A RAID ON THE INARTICULATE

Poet T. S. Eliot once likened writing a poem to conducting "a raid on the inarticulate."[29] I stumbled across that powerful image several years ago. It proceeded to lay dormant for a decade, but roused itself from a long hibernation one day as I pondered the Gospel of John's wonderful words about the incarnation of God:

> And the Word became flesh and lived among us . . . No one has ever seen God. It is God the only Son, who is close to the Father's heart, who has made [God] known. (vv. 14, 18)

The incarnation of God, the revelation of God in a human life, the flesh and blood life of Jesus, is the ultimate "raid on the inarticulate." The invisible God, whose reality can never be fully articulated, defined, or described, has come near in the incarnation. The Word of God, "what God means to say," was articulated, spoken, and revealed in a human life—the life of Jesus the Christ, the Son of God.

That is what the Gospel of John is about. Throughout John's Gospel, the recurring theme is that the life of Jesus is the best look we have ever had at God. It is difficult ground to cover, in a way. At times it seems as though the Jesus of John's Gospel makes no distinction between himself and God, while at other times the distinction between Jesus and God is clear. I have struggled with all that for as long as I can remember. Even as a child, when I heard people use the words "Jesus" and "God" interchangeably, I would wonder, "If Jesus is God, was heaven empty while Jesus was in Mary's womb and living on earth? If Jesus is God, who was Jesus praying to in Gethsemane and crying to on the cross? If Jesus is God, was God dead from Friday afternoon until Sunday morning?" Then one day I stumbled across that verse in Mark 10 where someone called Jesus "good," and Jesus replied, "Why do you call me good? No one is good but God alone" (v. 18). That only made my unspoken questions grow greater.

More sophisticated musings over those same questions have at times become the focus of "official Christianity." Major church councils and creeds have been convened and constructed in an effort to answer the "Christological question," the mystery of the relationship between Jesus and God. Significant examples of such efforts include the Council of Nicaea in 325, the Council of Constantinople in 381, and the Council of Chalcedon in 451. All of those doctrinal efforts and conciliar gatherings were related to the mystery of the incarnation of God, the revelation of God in the human life of Jesus.

To read the conclusions and creeds that emerged from those efforts is to begin to sense that some of what we call "orthodox doctrine" may actually be based more on those creeds and councils—sometimes called "historical theology" or "dogmatic theology"—than on the words of the four Gospels. That is not to say that the theology of dogma and doctrine is insignificant or unimportant. To ignore twenty centuries of theological development under the guise of "getting back to the Bible" would be foolish, wasteful, and lazy. That long theological evolution is our history, our heritage, and our foundation. We should study it and know it. But we should also remember that those who hammered out those conclusions were seekers and strugglers—a lot like all of us. And we should also consider the possibility that much of what we consider "orthodoxy" is based more on historical dogma than on the stark, unaveraged-out, words of the gospel. (A possible indicator of this may be that whenever we hear or read sermons that strike us as being "courageous," they are almost always sermons that go back most directly to the simple, unadorned words we find in the four gospels. That is ironic. Why does it strike us as "courageous" for someone to declare the simple gospel in church? Perhaps because what institutional churches (including noncreedal churches such as Baptists) accept as "orthodox belief" rests more on the creeds of the fourth century than on the Gospels of the first century. I don't know for sure, but I sense that it is so.)

This is rough ground to cross and uneven terrain to travel. There is mystery here: the eternal God, the divine Christ, the human Jesus. To try and speak of it feels like conducting an *unsuccessful* raid on inarticulate truth. But this much I believe: The life of Jesus is the ultimate revelation of God. When God got ready to have God's best Word with us, the Word that God gave came in the life of Jesus. And yet, if our confession is to be complete, we must also acknowledge that something of God was hidden in the same human life in which it was revealed.[30] After all, God is not human; God is God. And Jesus, the one human life that best showed us God, had his real human limits: He got tired. He got hungry. He did not know some things. Jesus was a full-time human being. In fact, we could say that the one who was the eternal Son of God was also the only fully human person who has ever lived. In Genesis, the word "human" was the name God gave to those who were created in God's image. If we let that be our definition of the word "human," then to be human means to live in the image of God, and Jesus is the only one who has ever absolutely, completely embodied the image of God. Thus, we can say, by the Bible's definition of the word "human," that Jesus is the only authentically human person who has ever lived.[31]

Because that is so, I wonder if it might also be so that the bread and cup of Holy Communion are signs of the Lord's life as well as the Lord's death, a sign of the whole body of Jesus (the incarnation) as well as the broken body of Jesus (the atonement). The crumbling crust of broken bread and the shimmering cup of something red call to mind our best glimpse of God, the glimpse of God we caught in the life of the only fully human person who ever lived—Jesus the Christ, who conducted the most clarifying raid of all on the most inarticulate Truth of all. Amen.

Lamb of God, Rose of Sharon, Prince of Peace—none of the things people have found to call him has ever managed to say it quite right. You can see why when he told people to follow him, they often did, even if they backed out later when they started to catch on to what lay ahead.

—Frederick Buechner
Peculiar Treasures

Long ago God spoke to our ancestors in many and various ways by the prophets, but in these last days, [God] has spoken to us by a Son . . .

—Hebrews 1:1-2

JESUS AND PAUL—
IN THAT ORDER

In Christ Jesus you are all children of God through faith. As many of you as were baptized into Christ have clothed yourselves with Christ. There is no longer Jew or Greek, there is no longer slave or free, there is no longer male or female; for all of you are one in Christ Jesus. (Gal 3:26-28)

That Paul, he sure knew how to make baptism deep and church radical! According to Paul, after someone is baptized, they belong to a new family. In this new family, race, social class, and gender exist, but they just don't count. Paul says that once the undiluted water of baptism gets in our eyes, we can no longer see any race, social class, or gender as being above or beneath any other race, class, or gender, for in Christ all are one in the new family of the baptized.

Those were some of the greatest words Paul ever wrote, but they are not the only words Paul ever wrote. There are other words, such as these from Corinthians: "Women should be silent in the churches. For they are not permitted to speak, but should be subordinate . . . For it is shameful for a woman to speak in church" (1 Cor 14:34-35). And, if you accept the traditional view that Paul wrote the pastoral epistles, there is this from 1 Timothy:

"Let a woman learn in silence with full submission. I permit no woman to teach or to have authority over a man; she is to keep silent" (2:11-12). And then there is this from Titus: "Tell slaves to be submissive to their masters" (2:9). In Galatians Paul says that all the boundary lines are washed away in the water of baptism. But, in other Bible books that are traditionally attributed to Paul, he acknowledges the boundaries and seems even to support them. So, what do you do?

Well, that depends on how you interpret the Bible. Some people interpret the Bible by what has been called "the ironing-board approach."[32] The ironing-board approach to scripture is based on the assumption that the Bible is as level and even as an ironing-board—no peaks, no valleys. This view of the Bible would assert that every word in scripture is equally authoritative for and applicable to our lives. That is the approach to the scripture on which many of us were nurtured. It is an approach to scripture with which many fine people are comfortable, but it has produced some strange and, at times, dreadful theology. For example, a prominent minister preached a series of sermons in the 1860s in which he sought to articulate a biblical defense of slavery. Taking the ironing-board approach to scripture, where every word in the Book is an everlastingly authoritative word straight from God, he found his biblical endorsement for enslaving human beings.

A more contemporary example of this approach to scripture can be found in the denominations and para-church groups that make much of the hierarchial approach to male and female relationships. If they say that they take up the matter of the submissive role of women because it is in the Bible and every word of scripture is authoritative for all time, then how do they justify jewelry and nice clothes and hair-dos, which, if every word of scripture is literally authoritative for all of life, are in defiance of 1 Timothy 2:9, which reads, "Women should dress . . . not with the hair braided, or with gold, pearls, or expensive clothes"? This is a problem if every word in the Bible is of equal significance, timelessness, and authority.

The truth is, the ironing-board approach to the Bible sounds good, but it won't hold up to the light of day. Would it not be better to just go ahead and say out loud that scripture has its peaks and valleys? I think people know intuitively that the Bible is not a flat ironing-board where all things are equal. People know that "women should be silent in the churches" is not on the same plane as "if God is for us, who is against us"? People know, intuitively, that "if a woman will not veil herself, then she should cut off her hair" is not exactly on the same pinnacle as "I am convinced that neither death, nor life, nor angels, nor rulers, nor things present, nor things to come, nor powers, nor height, nor depth, nor anything else in all creation, will be able to separate us from the love of God in Christ Jesus our Lord." People know, by the sanctified common sense of the children of God, that "if there is anything [wives] desire to know, let them ask their husbands at home" is not on the same ground as, "as many of you as were baptized into Christ have clothed yourselves with Christ. There is no longer Jew or Greek, there is no longer slave or free, there is no longer male or female." Does this mean that the Bible is littered with the debris of contradictions? No. It means that the Bible has peaks and valleys.

The peaks are timeless, universal truth for all people everywhere. The valleys are local, particular instructions for specific moments and places. Of course, when we say that out loud, it raises some tough questions: "But how do you know which is which? Who gets to decide which words are the lofty pinnacles that must guide and lead our behavior? What is the measure by which we are to interpret?"

I believe the answer is that, on those occasions when we interpret scripture, we should do our interpreting in the light of the life of Christ. If we believe that Jesus gives us our best look at God, then it is to the life of Jesus the Christ that we can look to find the measure by which to interpret scripture. This approach to scripture is clearly different from the ironing-board approach. Here is how it works: You read the four Gospels over and over until you develop an intuitive feel for the spirit of Christ, and then you measure truth in the light of what you know of Jesus.

If the life of Jesus has given us our best look at the way God means for life to be lived, and if the four Gospels have given us our best look at Jesus, then the four Gospels must be the center and measure by which scripture is interpreted. This does not place the four Gospels at the top of the Bible and everything else beneath them. Rather, this places the four Gospels at the center of the Bible and everything else around them. This is the Christocentric approach to scripture: Christ is at the center, and everything else is measured by the spirit of Christ, who is the measure of all things. This does not mean that we should "Christianize" the Hebrew scriptures and try to find Jesus in every prophecy and on every page. Rather, this means that when we read a scripture, for instance, that seems to bless revenge, we should ask of that scripture this question, "Is that true to the spirit of Christ?" Christ becomes, not the hidden message in the Hebrew scriptures, but the measure of practical application of scripture to our everyday lives.

This, for me, is the answer to the "How should we interpret Paul?" question. We should interpret Paul in the light of the life of Jesus. I believe that Paul would be the first to say, "Don't interpret Jesus in the light of my words; interpret my words in the light of Jesus." I believe Paul would be aghast at the vast, complicated, multilayered doctrinal maize in which the church wanders when it interprets Jesus in the light of Paul. Far better to interpret Paul in the light of Jesus, not because Paul contradicts Jesus, but because Jesus, not Paul, is the measure of ultimate truth.

That is how we can know that Galatians 3:28 is a towering pinnacle and lofty peak on the rolling landscape of sacred scripture. When we take the Christocentric approach to the Bible and saturate ourselves with the four Gospels by reading them over and over again, we come to know that Jesus saw all people as God's children created in God's image. Jesus defied his culture's conventional wisdom about social, racial, and gender superiority. He revealed his culture's conventional wisdom to be wrong, false, and sinful. Socially, he repeatedly aligned himself with the poor and struggling. Racially, he made it his business to have fellowship with Samaritans, the marginalized race of his culture. Regarding gender, he never gave any gift to a man that he didn't give to a woman.[33] That is the way Jesus was, and if the way Jesus was is our best look at the way God is, then we know that when Paul says that in Christ we have been baptized into a new family where race, class, and gender don't count, we are standing on a peak, walking on a mountain, perched on a tower at the top of a hill. Measured by the spirit of Christ, Paul's words about the new family ring true all the way to the center of who we are.

That is an example of the practical outcome of the Christocentric approach to scripture. It is obviously very different from the "ironing-board" approach to the Bible. Stated simply, it says there is a question that is more important than the "Is something biblical?" question, and that question is to ask if something is true to the spirit of Christ. That, of course, can be a rather subjective question and, thus, raises the specter of the proverbial "slippery-slope."

Once we start interpreting the Bible in the light of the spirit of Christ, aren't we on a very subjective "slippery-slope"? Yes, absolutely. To decide to interpret scripture in the light of the spirit of Christ is to venture out on a risky slippery-slope. But the truth is, everyone is already on the slippery-slope. Everyone has already ventured out into the perils of biblical interpretation, because no one embraces the idea that God would approve stoning a stubborn child (Deut 21:18-21) or giving the death penalty to someone for picking up sticks on the Sabbath (Num 15:32-36). Once we leave the ironing-board, we are on the slippery-slope.

And anyway, there is great company out there on that slippery-slope. After all, that is where Jesus led us when he said those words in John 14:25, "I have said these things to you while I am still with you. But the Advocate, the Holy Spirit, whom the Father will send in my name, will teach you everything, and remind you of all that I have said to you," and in John 16:13, "When the Spirit of truth comes, he will guide you into all the truth." With those words Jesus put us on the slippery-slope of interpreting scripture, truth, and gospel by the inner nudges and quiet tugs of the Holy Spirit who would remind us of what Jesus revealed about God. That is the gloriously risky place where Jesus dropped us off on his way home. It can feel perilous, and it can be mysterious. The slippery-slope is not as neat and easy as the ironing-board. But for me at least, it seems to be more true to the spirit of Jesus and, for that matter, the spirit of Paul—in that order. Amen.

I take it as a first principle that we must not interpret any one part of Scripture so that it contradicts other parts, and specially we must not use an apostle's teaching to contradict that of our Lord.

—C. S. Lewis
Letters of C. S. Lewis

I still have many things to say to you,
but you cannot bear them now.
When the Spirit of truth comes,
he will guide you into all the truth.

—John 16:12-13

IF JESUS CAME TO TOWN

If Jesus came to your town, where would he go to church? The last time Jesus was in town, he went to worship at the synagogue. So I imagine that, based on what Jesus did when he was here before, he would worship God with a Jewish congregation on Saturdays. But what about on other days? Where do you suppose Jesus would go to church if Jesus came to your town?

I think I saw a Jesus kind of church a decade ago. It happened while I was waiting to see a patient in a nursing home. I was standing out in the hall, where I happened to be positioned directly beneath a loud speaker through which, with no warning, there came an announcement I will never forget. Sounding for all the world like a line out of a Flannery O'Connor short story, the announcement declared, "The Church of God has come and is waiting for you in the Pine Room."

Since my patient was still occupied, I decided to journey down to the Pine Room and see if a visiting congregation had come to lead vespers or if judgment day had come and somebody had forgotten to tell me. When I rounded the corner of the corridor that led to the Pine Room, I saw a sight so sacred that it has remained to this day frozen in time. There, before me, was the Pine Room, a darkly-paneled sitting room turned sanctuary.

The sun was streaming in through a venetian blind, and there in the slanting beams of the afternoon was the worship leader from the Church of God. Her high bun of never-cut hair and her face with no make-up were sure signs of her heritage. She was leading the congregation in the singing of "What a Friend We Have in Jesus." The congregation consisted of the piano player from the Church of God and an old man in a wheelchair. He was parked right in front of the song leader, a wide white strap of cloth keeping him in, a thin brown stripe of snuff creasing his chin.

I stood there at the edge of their holy place, paralyzed by the unspeakable beauty of the children of God at worship in the Pine Room. Even the dust that floated in the sunbeams seemed to become a host of miniature angels, line-dancing in festal array. The world stopped turning. And over the strains of "What a Friend We Have in Jesus," I heard a voice from somewhere far above me or somewhere deep inside me say, "If Jesus came to town, this is probably where Jesus would go to church; among the powerless and meek who serve on the margins and from the edges of the forgotten corners of life."

Where do you think Jesus might go to church if he came to your town? What sort of church would be pleasing to Jesus? If we trim the gospel down to the size of our prevailing American culture, we can create a Jesus with whom we can feel pretty much at home. Standard North American religion says that we have a Jesus who would want the church to become a successful institution, a Jesus who is pleased by a church that gains power and acquires status. That is the sort of popular religion that shaped my consciousness for the first thirty years of my life. I had so thoroughly Americanized Jesus that I just naturally assumed that what my culture valued, Jesus valued. But then I slipped up one day and started reading the Gospels. Too much exposure to the

Gospels will ruin a person for our culture's standard assumptions about what constitutes a "successful" church.

When I was growing up, whenever anybody went away to seminary, we usually sent them off with the familiar chorus of "Don't let 'em ruin you." That's what folks where I come from frequently said to preachers when they went off to college or seminary to study theology and scripture. "Don't let'em ruin you!" we'd say, which meant, "Don't learn a bunch of stuff that's going to change you and cause you to get notions and come back with troubling new perspectives on things we've already settled."

I think there was more truth in our well-intentioned warning than we knew. If the phrase, "Don't let 'em ruin you" means, essentially, "Don't let them show you so much about the gospel that it changes you," then I think our warning was absolutely on target. In fact, if someone ever says to you, "I've decided that I'm going to read Matthew, Mark, Luke, and John all the way through several times in the coming year," you might want to say to them, "Well that's fine, but, don't let 'em ruin you." Because they can—and they will.

Matthew, Mark, Luke, and John are without a doubt the most dangerous Gospel quartet that ever got together. If you think you want to saturate your life with what they have to say, you might want to pause a moment and be sure. After all, if you are looking for something safe, comfortable, conventional, and manageable, you might not want to rummage around too long in the four Gospels. They can ruin you. They can ruin you for our popular North American version of the gospel that makes Jesus sound like an advocate of our comfortable materialism. They can certainly ruin you for invoking the name of Jesus to bless everything we happen to think is nice or proper or good. And the ruination is cumulative! The more you read them, the more they ruin you!

I keep hoping the four Gospels might change—you know, lighten up a little—but not so. No matter how many times you read the Gospels, Jesus still has nowhere to lay his head. He still sends his people out without so much as a second pair of sandals. He still says sell your possessions and give the proceeds to the poor. Jesus would probably look for a church to belong to that embodies such principles, what with those being his principles and all. (Maybe some place simple and sacred, like the Church of God in the Pine Room.) I wonder what it would be like to be in the same church with Jesus. I don't think I'm up to it.

To read the four Gospels is to begin to sense that we might need to rethink what we believe about church and institutional Christianity. The four Gospels just will not let us hold on to a vision of church that measures success and worth by the prevailing standards of North American culture. The Jesus of the four Gospels appears to be looking for followers who gladly and freely spend themselves, give themselves away and make themselves vulnerable for the sake for those who are least, last, and struggling. I could even see Jesus getting excited about a church that sold off its assets and literally gave itself entirely away, worked itself right out of business, only to start over in a little pocket here and a little pocket there. (It's a silly notion, but it struck me while I was reading the Gospels.)

Read the four Gospels, if you dare. But wear a crash helmet, and buckle both snaps on your chinstrap. Too much exposure to Matthew, Mark, Luke, and John can ruin you for the conventional wisdom that shapes our assumptions about many things, even (or especially) what constitutes a "successful" church. Amen.

It is madness to wear . . . straw hats and velvet hats to church;
   we should all be wearing crash helmets.
Ushers should issue life preservers and signal flares;
   they should lash us to our pews.

—Annie Dillard
"An Expedition to the Pole"

When [Jesus] came to Nazareth, where he had been brought up, he went to the synagogue on the sabbath day, as was his custom. He stood up to read, and the scroll of the prophet Isaiah was given to him. He unrolled the scroll and found the place where it was written: "The Spirit of the Lord is upon me, because he has annointed me to bring good news to the poor. He has sent me to proclaim release to the captives and recovery of sight to the blind, to let the oppressed go free, to proclaim the year of the Lord's favor."

And he rolled up the scroll, gave it back to the attendant, and sat down. The eyes of all in the synagogue were fixed on him. Then he began so say to them, "Today this scripture has been fulfilled in your hearing."

—Luke 4:16-21

BETWEEN JESUS AND THE CHURCH

I f we read the Gospels honestly, it is, as Annie Dillard once suggested, an exercise to be undertaken more in a crash helmet
than a bonnet.[34] An honest reading of the Gospels can be a rough
ride. An honest effort at hearing the words of the four Gospels
will eventually leave you with the sense that there is a troubling
gap of distance between Jesus and the church. You would like, of
course, to think that Jesus and the church are always arm in arm,
shoulder to shoulder, "traveling along, singing a song, side by
side." After all, the church is only in the world to be the body of
Christ. And the Bible does say that Jesus is the head of the body,
the church's one and only Lord. So, you would like to assume
that Jesus and the church are right together, all the time,
everywhere.

And yet, when you read the four Gospels over and over again,
and you look at the church as it has evolved over these twenty
centuries, you cannot help but sense that here and there, now
and then, there is a gap between the church's Lord and the Lord's
church. The temptation, of course, is to cast a nostalgic gaze to
the past and say that it is the modern church that has failed to
keep up with Jesus and that, in the good old days, there was no
gap of distance between Jesus and the church. That, however, is

a temptation to be resisted. The gap between Jesus and the church is not new. Indeed, it is about as old as the church itself. You can't even get through the books of Acts, Galatians, Corinthians, and Philippians without encountering tales of fragmentation, manipulation, jealousy, and unkindness in the body of Christ. The church can't make it through its infancy without stumbling off in strange directions that open up a gap of space between Jesus and the church. But that, of course, should not strike us as too odd. After all, there is a gap between the absolute integrity and unfailing courage of Jesus and every person who has ever lived. And since churches are, after all, collections of people, it should come as no surprise that from the beginning there has been this bothersome gap of distance between Jesus and the church.

The gap between Jesus and the church has been more noticeable at some times than at others. In the fourth century, for example, when Constantine converted to Christianity and gave the church his imperial blessing, the church began to receive official favors. No longer a persecuted sect, Christianity became a sanctioned religion toward which the emperor tilted money for the construction of impressive church buildings. That sounds like a fine position for the church to enjoy, until you look at the four Gospels and see a Jesus who lived in utter simplicity, without a place to lay his head, without an ounce of political power or material acquisition.

There was a gap between the imperial church of the fourth century, with its nationalistic alliances and its material successes, and the simple Jesus who came for all the people of all nations and who called his followers to go on their mission without so much as an extra pair of shoes. All of which reminds us that any gap between Jesus and the church is not a new development, a recent invention, or a contemporary emergence in the history of the church. I suppose you could say that as long as there has been a church, there has been a gap between the words and works of Jesus and the church that is in the world only to be the body of Christ, living out the spirit of Jesus.

That spirit of Jesus is nowhere stated more clearly than in Luke 4. Jesus, reading in the synagogue, said:

> The spirit of the Lord is upon me, because he has anointed me to bring good news to the poor. He has sent me to proclaim release to the captives and recovery of sight to the blind, to let the oppressed go free. (v. 18)

When Jesus finished reading those words, he said, "Today this scripture has been fulfilled in your hearing" (v. 19), which means, "This scripture is the scripture that defines what I have come to do." Jesus defined his reason for being in the world with the words of Isaiah:

> The spirit of the Lord God is upon me, because the Lord has anointed me; he has sent me to bring good news to the oppressed, to bind up the brokenhearted, to proclaim liberty to the captives, and release to the prisoners. (61:1)

That is how Jesus defined his mission, and a careful reading of the four Gospels shows Jesus fulfilling that mission by giving himself away in acts of healing, righteousness, and love. This means, of course, that the church should do the same. If the church is the body of Christ and Christ is the head of the body, then the church's model for its mission and purpose should be found in the words and works of Jesus.

But that model is not always easy to embrace, is it? The pull of our culture tugs so hard. For the church to embody the spirit of Jesus, it must live against the times and go against the tide. The tide of our times and the tug of our world push the church to measure itself by the prevailing standards of North American culture, which leads churches to become consumed with such things as size, power, and prominence—none of which reflects the standards by which Jesus measured life, but all of which reflect the values by which our culture measures life.

When churches embrace their culture's measures of worth and success, a gap seems to grow between Jesus and the church. On one hand, we have the simple Jesus, whose life was turned outward; the simple Jesus who never acquired anything, but lived to spend himself for the sake of the Kingdom of God. On the other hand, we have the church that, especially in twentieth-century North America, feels the tug of the culture that measures worth by size and power. When the church adopts those measures as its own, success becomes the goal to be achieved. Once success becomes the church's goal, people become commodities to be gotten. Once people become commodities to be gotten, other churches become competitors to be outdone. Once other churches become competitors to be outdone, then the gospel becomes a product to be marketed. Once the gospel becomes a product to be marketed, then the gap is pretty wide between the church that is turned inward to seek its own success and the Jesus who was turned outward to find the least and the last and the lost to tell them and show them and give them the love of God.

The tug of our culture is hard to resist. And we are all so much the children of our culture that we sometimes don't even know there is a gap between the way Jesus spent his life and the way churches spend their lives. And even when we do recognize the gap between Jesus and the church, it is no easy matter to define it, much less shrink it.

Here is a practical example. Sometimes we read about state-of-the-art multipurpose gymnasiums that churches construct. In the same cities where such facilities are constructed there are homeless people. I wonder if Jesus would say, "If you have so many dollars, and you feel inclined to build something, don't build one 'family life center,' build fifty! Build fifty centers of family life. Build fifty Habitat for Humanity houses in my name to help put a decent roof over the heads of God's children." Sometimes I wonder.

But it's not that simple because some very good things happen in enormous, expensive, church facilities. I cannot level a sweeping indictment against all such undertakings. I have too many beams in my own eye to be picking specks from anyone else's. For example, I am partial to stained glass. I find it beautiful to the eye and moving to the soul. But I sometimes wonder, on bitter midwinter midnights, if somewhere a crimson-and-blue Jesus gazes out over some city's homeless children and tries to climb down. I wonder if all the stained-glass-Jesuses whisper urgently from their lofty perches, "Get us down from here! Cash us in. Spend us on the street for housing and medicine and food and jackets for God's poor!" I don't know. This is not simple. After all, beauty itself is sacred. Plus, that would mean turning masonry into bakery, turning stones into bread. Once, Jesus declined to do such a thing. So who can know what is the answer? I certainly don't have the answer, but I do have the question. The church should at least have the question.

How do you reconcile the simple Jesus with much of what our world would call "the successful church?" Think about it. In our culture people generally look at the churches with the most expansive holdings and enormous crowds and equate that with God's blessing. Yet those were not the standards Jesus invoked to measure his mission. In fact, once when Jesus looked up and saw a huge crowd following him, he said, "You all might want to stop and think about this. Before you join up, you might want to count the cost because to follow me will mean to deny yourself and take up the cross." (Jesus had obviously never attended a church growth conference, or he would have known that is not the way it is done!)

This is not simple. The gap between Jesus and the church is, to some degree, inevitable. After all, we don't live in first-century Palestine. We cannot all be Jewish carpenters who live beneath the stars. A part of the gap between Jesus and the church is the gap between the first century and the twentieth century. (Jesus once found his followers netting the surf; now he has followers surfing the net.) There is nothing bothersome about that gap; it is the natural, inevitable, progressive gap of time. What is bothersome, troubling, and complex is the gap of spirit—the gap between the spirit of Jesus and the life of the church. The only way to face that gap and shrink that gap is for the church to measure what it does by the standard of the spirit of Jesus.

We have to be careful with all of this. For one thing, we have to be careful lest we leap to the conclusion that small, simple churches are always nearer to the spirit of Jesus than huge, imposing churches. That is an oversimplification that doesn't always prove true. God is doing good things in many places, large and elaborate as well as small and simple. Another reason we have to be careful with all this talk about the gap between Jesus and the church is that it can easily harden into an exaggerated dismay over the modern church's failures and a jaded cynicism about the institutional church's future. The truth is, the church is the body of Christ; a wounded body, perhaps; a scarred, some-times-lagging-behind body, but the body of Christ nonetheless. And the world would be indescribably the poorer without the gospel the church proclaims and the deeds the church does and the love of Christ the church shows.

There is a gap between the spirit of Jesus and the life of the church. Always has been. Always will be. But even so, when the church is at its best, it can be among the best demonstrations of God's kingdom that this world will ever see. And when are we at our best? When we are most true to the spirit of Jesus. And when are we most true to the spirit of Jesus? Well, according to Jesus, when we bring good news to the poor, bind up the broken, liberate the oppressed, feed the hungry, visit the lonely, clothe the naked, defend the powerless, embrace the hurting, and shelter the weak. When we are most turned outward, we are most true to the spirit of our Lord. And as for that gap between Jesus and the church . . . well, maybe it shrinks a little. Who knows? Maybe there are fleeting moments when we even catch up a little to the One we are following. Amen.

It doesn't really matter
whether an action is profitable or popular,
whether it is practical or realistic,
whether it wins a salute from a city or nation.
What matters only and always is
whether it can be understood as following Jesus.
—Ernest Campbell
"Follow Me"

[Jesus] called the crowd with his disciples, and said to them,
"If any want to become my followers,
let them deny themselves
and take up their cross
and follow me."
—Mark 8:34

ALTARS TO THE WIND

Emily Dickinson once wrote, "The vane defines the wind."[35] She was speaking, of course, of those spinning rooftop adornments that once dotted the countryside. Weather vanes turn in whatever direction the breeze is blowing, thus they "define the wind," said the famous nineteenth-century American poet. A hundred years later the famous twentieth-century American poet, Garth Brooks, almost echoed Emily when he gathered several of his ballads beneath the intriguing phrase, "roping the wind."[36]

"Defining the wind" and "roping the wind": Now that's a pair of phrases Nicodemus could have put to good use the night he came to visit Jesus. When Jesus told Nicodemus that he needed to be born from above, Nicodemus (not surprisingly) found that a bewildering notion, so he pressed Jesus for an explanation, to which Jesus replied that the ways of God with the lives of people are like the wind. You cannot explain the wind, predict the wind, catch, corral, or manage the wind. It blows where it chooses. And that, Jesus told Nicodemus, is the way it is with everyone who is born of the Spirit. At that point Nicodemus probably should have just dropped his jaw and said, "Wow!" Instead, he furrowed his brow and said, "How?" "How can these things be?" Nicodemus wanted some answers. Lacking sufficient lassoes to rope the wind and tie it down, he at least wanted a weather vane to define the wind and nail it down.

We sort of like Nicodemus because we are sort of like Nicodemus: We, too, could use a little more clarity, explanation, and light. John 3 reports that Nicodemus came to Jesus at night, which in John's Gospel is usually a sign of bewilderment, confusion, or mystery—a sign of "being in the dark." Because he was in the dark, Nicodemus sought answers, explanations, definitions. His spirit lives on in every generation. It is the healthy spirit of the curious seeker and the honest struggler. Across the centuries it has been the curious seekers and honest strugglers who have constructed the confessions, established the doctrines, and articulated the ideas that have become what people now call "orthodox Christianity." Those ideas, confessions, and doctrines are the handles by which we hold onto the invisible, untouchable God. We cannot manage, control, or predict the wind of God's Spirit. As Jesus said, it blows where and how it will. So, lacking sufficient rope to weave the wind a halter, we assemble sufficient words to build the wind an altar. Doctrines, creeds, confessions, convictions—all of those are our best efforts to hold onto our experience of God. They are our altars to the wind.

In his poem, "The Rock," T. S. Eliot sings to God a wonderful hymn that is about all of this:

> O Light Invisible, we praise Thee!
> Too bright for mortal vision . . .
> We thank Thee for our little light that is
>   dappled with shadow . . .
>
> And when we have built an altar
>   to the Invisible Light, we may
> Set thereon the little lights for which our
>   bodily vision is made.[37]

T. S. Eliot says that since our eyes are not able to see the Invisible Light of God, we do the next best thing: we build altars to the Invisible Light and place on those altars we have made the little lights we can see. It's true, isn't it? God is God—Light Invisible, Wind Unmanageable. We build altars to the wind: confessions, creeds, convictions, the reformed tradition, the Baptist principles, Methodism, Pentecostalism, Catholicism, what Augustine said, what John Calvin said, what Martin Luther said, premillennialism, postmillennialism. The long line of altars to the wind winds its way across the centuries, all the way from now back to that night when Nicodemus asked Jesus, "How can these things be?" Jesus said, "It's like the wind," and ever since we've been busy defining the wind, roping the wind, explaining the wind, building altars to the wind.

The altars are helpful. We have to have them. But somehow we have to remember what came before them. We have to remember, for instance, that when the little New Testament book of Jude speaks of "the faith that was once and for all entrusted to the saints," it is not talking about the vast array of orthodox doctrine collected over twenty centuries of altar building. The faith once and for all delivered to the saints is the truth of the gospel of Jesus Christ, the good story of the wind of God's Spirit that gives us a new birth to a whole new way of life. Somehow we have to look behind all our altars to the wind and remember what we had before our vast religious infrastructure evolved.

And beyond that, think of this: Even the written Gospel accounts that preceded all of our later altars to the wind are themselves altars to the wind. After all, Jesus and Nicodemus had their late night conversation on a breezy evening around 30 AD. The Gospel of John was not written until about sixty years later. The death and resurrection of Jesus happened in the early thirties. So why was Mark written in the mid-sixties, Matthew and

Luke perhaps in the seventies, and John even a bit later? To hold onto the memory of the experience of Jesus before it slipped away . . . To keep it, so the story could keep going. After all, the original eyewitnesses were dying, and the earliest followers were being scattered to the four winds. The story that had been experienced and repeated had to be preserved and held onto. And what if no one had written it down? Our lives would be immeasurably, unspeakably, tragically the poorer if the Gospels had not been written and preserved. But the wind of God would still have blown, and it would still be blowing. Even the wonderful, inspired, inspiring, beautiful Bible books are altars to the wind. There is even something behind and before the written words of scripture. The wind of God blew long before anyone ever wrote it down, and it would still be blowing even if there had never been written a single word of sacred scripture.

I once heard Furman University religion professor Jeffrey Rogers invoke an image that I will never forget. Concerning those who cannot be content to just repeat what conventional religious wisdom tells them to say, Dr. Rogers said this: "Some people have a calling from God to be theological test pilots. They have to fly out to the edge and see what is over the horizon. It is their calling. It is dangerous work, being a theological test pilot. Some of them fly out over the horizon and keep going. They never come back."

I've known a theological test pilot or two in my life. (Come to think of it, I haven't seen them lately!) Though I myself am more of a theological cropduster, even I have seen far enough over the horizon to know that what we call "orthodox religion" is a series of altars we have built to the wind we have felt. If we fly out to the horizon and look over the edge, what we see is what lies beyond all our altars to the wind. And wonder of wonders, what lies *beyond* our altars to the wind is the same thing that came *before* our altars to the wind. It is the Spirit of God, giving new birth and new life to those who trust themselves to it and cast themselves upon it. It is a wind that cannot be defined by any vane or caught in any rope. It is the wind that blew long before all of our systems of doctrine and denomination were ever articulated, the wind that would still be blowing even if they had never been established. To acknowledge that is not to deny the place of our systems of doctrine and denomination; it is, rather, to confess that they are not the guardians of captured truth—just altars to ultimate truth.

We have to have those altars; they are the only handles we have for holding onto the One we cannot touch, hold, or contain. We are like Mary in the garden on the morning of the resurrection. She yearned to hold onto the Risen Lord. But the Risen Lord said it could not be done. The Risen Lord told Mary she would have to let go. We find that too frightening, too difficult, too uncertain, too mystical, too unsure. We have to have handles for holding on. We need definitions and explanations. We don't do well without them. But somehow we have to recover the truth that they are only the small altars on which we set our little lights, "dappled with shadow." Denominationalism, orthodoxy, doctrinal requirements . . . They all have their place, but when we finally enter into the unhindered, uninterrupted, unending, presence of God, they will . . .

> Have their day and cease to be,
> They are but broken lights of Thee
> And Thou, O Lord art more than they.
> Amen

Jesus said that the Spirit of God is like the wind, blowing wherever it wants, transcending reason and explanation. Ever since Jesus said that, we have all been busy building denominational fences through which to channel the wind, fashioning orthodox boxes in which to corral the wind, erecting doctrinal fortresses from which to defend the wind. I sometimes wonder if God might have preferred for us just to hang out a wind-chime.

—Charles E. Poole

*The wind blows where it chooses,
and you hear the sound of it,
but you do not know where it comes from or where it goes.
So it is with everyone who is born of the Spirit.*

—John 3:8

NOTES

[1] *T. S. Eliot, The Complete Poems and Plays* (New York: Harcourt Brace and Co., 1980) 128.

[2] "Something breaks through language and escapes" was a favorite phrase of the late John W. Carlton, which he attributed to Robert Browning.

[3] *Alfred Lord Tennyson, Selected Poems*, Aidan Day, ed. (New York: Penguin Books, 1991) 130.

[4] Lyrics by Gary Nicholson (New York: Sony/Epic Records, 1996).

[5] A phrase I heard attributed to Ernest Campbell.

[6] For a helpful treatment of Pharisees and scribes, see the article "Pharisees," *Mercer Dictionary of the Bible*, Watson Mills, ed. (Macon GA: Mercer University Press, 1990) 680.

[7] Helen Sheehy and Leslie Stainton, *On Writers and Writing* (Korea: Tide-mark Press, 1995).

[8] *Selected Poems and Letters of Emily Dickinson*, Robert N. Linscott, ed. (New York: Anchor Books, 1959) 150.

[9] Source unknown.

[10] *A Chorus of Witnesses*, Thomas G. Long and Cornelius Platinga, Jr., eds. (Grand Rapids: Wm. B. Eerdmans, 1994) 264.

[11] For this sentence I am indebted to a convergence of thoughts from John Killinger and C. S. Lewis.

[12] The phrase "getting God in our debt" is not original with me, but I cannot cite its birthplace.

[13]Barbara Brown Taylor, *The Preaching Life* (Boston: Cowley Publications, 1993) 9.

[14]Frederick Buechner, *Wishful Thinking* (New York: HarperCollins Publishers, 1993) 30.

[15]Halford Luccock published a book many years ago called *Marching Off the Map*.

[16]Adapted from Thomas G. Long, *Hebrews in Interpretation* (Louisville KY: John Knox Press, 1997) 3.

[17]Frederick Buechner, *A Room Called Remember* (San Francisco: Harper and Row, 1984) 34.

[18]From an unpublished sermon by Fred Craddock.

[19]As quoted in Charles Poole, *The Tug of Home* (Macon GA: Smyth and Helwys Publishing, Inc., 1997) 29.

[20]A statement I heard spoken by Walter B. Shurden.

[21]*Listening for God*, Paula J. Carlson and Peter S. Hawkins, eds. (Minneapolis: Augsburg Fortress, 1994) 119.

[22]Adapted from Annie Dillard, *The Annie Dillard Reader* (New York: HarperCollins, 1994) 447.

[23]Elizabeth Barrett Browning, *Aurora Leigh and Other Poems*, John Robert Glorney Bolton and Julia Bolton Holloway, eds. (London: Penguin Books, 1995) 232.

[24]Thornton Wilder, *Our Town* (New York: Harper and Row, 1938) 99-100.

[25]Adapted from Bruce Larson, *The Communicator's Commentary: Luke* (Waco TX: Word Books, 1983) 46.

[26]D. H. Lawrence, "The Hands of God," as quoted in Andrew J. Good's "Fear of Falling" in *Best Sermons*, James W. Cox, ed. (New York: HarperCollins, 1990) 229.

[27]I heard R. Kirby Godsey use this phrase in a public prayer many years ago.

[28]Quoted in Charles B. Bugg, *A Faith To Meet Our Fears* (Macon GA: Smyth and Helwys Publishing, Inc., 1996).

[29]*T. S. Eliot*, 128.

[30]See Fred Craddock, *Preaching* (Nashville: Abingdon Press, 1985) 56-57.

[31]See Dale Moody, *The Word of Truth* (Grand Rapids: Eerdmans, 1981) 419.

[32]For the phrase "ironing-board approach" I am indebted to the late Dale Moody, whom I heard use the phrase in a sermon many years ago.

[33]For this sentence I am indebted to John Claypool, whom I heard say a similar statement at Mercer University's Theological Institute in the 1980s.

[34]Dillard, 38.

[35]Linscott, 323.

[36]*Ropin' the Wind*, Garth Brooks (Nashville: Garthart, Inc. and Caged Panther Music, Inc./Capitol Records, 1991).

[37]*T. S. Eliot*, 112-14.

Other available titles from

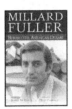

Beyond the American Dream
Millard Fuller

In 1968, Millard finished the story of his journey from pauper to millionaire to home builder. His wife, Linda, occasionally would ask him about getting it published, but Millard would reply, "Not now. I'm too busy." This is that story. *978-1-57312-563-5 272 pages/pb* **$20.00**

Blissful Affliction
The Ministry and Misery of Writing
Judson Edwards

Edwards draws from more than forty years of writing experience to explore why we use the written word to change lives and how to improve the writing craft. *978-1-57312-594-9 144 pages/pb* **$15.00**

Choosing Gratitude
Learning to Love the Life You Have
James A. Autry

Autry reminds us that gratitude is a choice, a spiritual—not social—process. He suggests that if we cultivate gratitude as a way of being, we may not change the world and its ills, but we can change our response to the world. If we fill our lives with moments of gratitude, we will indeed love the life we have. *978-1-57312-614-4 144 pages/pb* **$15.00**

Contextualizing the Gospel
A Homiletic Commentary on 1 Corinthians
Brian L. Harbour

Harbour examines every part of Paul's letter, providing a rich resource for those who want to struggle with the difficult texts as well as the simple texts, who want to know how God's word—all of it—intersects with their lives today. *978-1-57312-589-5 240 pages/pb* **$19.00**

Dance Lessons
Moving to the Beat of God's Heart
Jeanie Miley

Miley shares her joys and struggles a she learns to "dance" with the Spirit of the Living God. *978-1-57312-622-9 240 pages/pb* **$19.00**

To order call **1-800-747-3016** or visit **www.helwys.com**

Daniel (Smyth & Helwys Annual Bible Study series)
Keeping Faith When the Heat Is On
Bill Ireland

Daniel is a book about resistance. It was written to people under pressure. In the book, we will see the efforts oppressive regimes take to undermine the faith and identity of God's people. In it, we will also see the strategies God's people employed in resisting the imposition of a foreign culture, and we will see what sustained their efforts. In that vein, the book of Daniel is powerfully relevant. *Teaching Guide 978-1-57312-647-2 144 pages/pb* **$14.00**

Study Guide 978-1-57312-646-5 80 pages/pb **$6.00**

A Divine Duet
Ministry and Motherhood
Alicia Davis Porterfield, ed.

Each essay in this inspiring collection is as different as the mother-minister who wrote it, from theologians to chaplains, inner-city ministers to rural-poverty ministers, youth pastors to preachers, mothers who have adopted, birthed, and done both.

978-1-57312-676-2 146 pages/pb **$16.00**

Divorce Ministry
A Guidebook
Charles Qualls

This book shares with the reader the value of establishing a divorce recovery ministry while also offering practical insights on establishing your own unique church-affiliated program. Whether you are working individually with one divorced person or leading a large group, *Divorce Ministry: A Guidebook* provides helpful resources to guide you through the emotional and relational issues divorced people often encounter.

978-1-57312-588-8 156 pages/pb **$16.00**

The Enoch Factor
The Sacred Art of Knowing God
Steve McSwain

The Enoch Factor is a persuasive argument for a more enlightened religious dialogue in America, one that affirms the goals of all religions—guiding followers in self-awareness, finding serenity and happiness, and discovering what the author describes as "the sacred art of knowing God." *978-1-57312-556-7 256 pages/pb* **$21.00**

Healing Our Hurts
Coping with Difficult Emotions

Daniel Bagby

In *Healing Our Hurts*, Daniel Bagby identifies and explains all the dynamics at play in these complex emotions. Offering practical biblical insights to these feelings, he interprets faith-based responses to separate overly religious piety from true, natural human emotion. This book helps us learn how to deal with life's difficult emotions in a redemptive and responsible way.

978-1-57312-613-7 144 pages/pb **$15.00**

Hope for the Thinking Christian
Seeking a Path of Faith through Everyday Life

Stephen Reese

Readers who want to confront their faith more directly, to think it through and be open to God in an individual, authentic, spiritual encounter will find a resonant voice in Stephen Reese.

978-1-57312-553-6 160 pages/pb **$16.00**

A Hungry Soul Desperate to Taste God's Grace
Honest Prayers for Life

Charles Qualls

Part of how we *see* God is determined by how we *listen* to God. There is so much noise and movement in the world that competes with images of God. This noise would drown out God's beckoning voice and distract us. Charles Qualls's newest book offers readers prayers for that journey toward the meaning and mystery of God. 978-1-57312-648-9 152 pages/pb **$14.00**

James M. Dunn and Soul Freedom
Aaron Douglas Weaver

James Milton Dunn, over the last fifty years, has been the most aggressive Baptist proponent for religious liberty in the United States. Soul freedom—voluntary, uncoerced faith and an unfettered individual conscience before God—is the basis of his understanding of church-state separation and the historic Baptist basis of religious liberty.

978-1-57312-590-1 224 pages/pb **$18.00**

The Jesus Tribe
Following Christ in the Land of the Empire

Ronnie McBrayer

The Jesus Tribe fleshes out the implications, possibilities, contradictions, and complexities of what it means to live within the Jesus Tribe and in the shadow of the American Empire.

978-1-57312-592-5 208 pages/pb **$17.00**

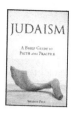

Judaism
A Brief Guide to Faith and Practice
Sharon Pace

Sharon Pace's newest book is a sensitive and comprehensive intro-duction to Judaism. What is it like to be born into the Jewish community? How does belief in the One God and a universal morality shape the way in which Jews see the world? How does one find meaning in life and the courage to endure suffering? How does one mark joy and forge com-munity ties?

978-1-57312-644-1 144 pages/pb **$16.00**

Lessons from the Cloth 2
501 More One Minute Motivators for Leaders
Bo Prosser and Charles Qualls

As the force that drives organizations to accomplishment, leader-ship is at a crucial point in churches, corporations, families, and almost every arena of life. Without leadership there is chaos. *With* leadership there is sometimes chaos! In this follow-up to their first volume, Bo Prosser and Charles Qualls will inspire you to keep growing in your leadership career.

978-1-57312-665-6 152 pages/pb **$11.00**

Let Me More of Their Beauty See
Reading Familiar Verses in Context
Diane G. Chen

Let Me More of Their Beauty See offers eight examples of how atten-tion to the historical and literary settings can safeguard against taking a text out of context, bring out its transforming power in greater dimension, and help us apply Scripture appropriately in our daily lives.

978-1-57312-564-2 160 pages/pb **$17.00**

Looking Around for God
The Strangely Reverent Observations of an Unconventional Christian
James A. Autry

Looking Around for God, Autry's tenth book, is in many ways his most personal. In it he considers his unique life of faith and belief in God. Autry is a former Fortune 500 executive, author, poet, and consultant whose work has had a significant influence on leadership thinking.

978-157312-484-3 144 pages/pb **$16.00**

Maggie Lee for Good

Jinny and John Hinson

Maggie Lee for Good captures the essence of a young girl's boundless faith and spirit. Her parents' moving story of the accident that took her life will inspire readers who are facing loss, looking for evidence of God's sustaining grace, or searching for ways to make a meaningful difference in the lives of others.   *978-1-57312-630-4 144 pages/pb* **$15.00**

Making the Timeless Word Timely

A Primer for Preachers

Michael B. Brown

Michael Brown writes, "There is a simple formula for sermon preparation that creates messages that apply and engage whether your parish is rural or urban, young or old, rich or poor, five thousand members or fifty." The other part of the task, of course, involves being creative and insightful enough to know how to take the general formula for sermon preparation and make it particular in its impact on a specific congregation. Brown guides the reader through the formula and the skills to employ it with excellence and integrity.   *978-1-57312-578-9 160 pages/pb* **$16.00**

Meeting Jesus Today

For the Cautious, the Curious, and the Committed

Jeanie Miley

Meeting Jesus Today, ideal for both individual study and small groups, is intended to be used as a workbook. It is designed to move readers from studying the Scriptures and ideas within the chapters to recording their journey with the Living Christ.

978-1-57312-677-9 320 pages/pb **$19.00**

The Ministry Life

101 Tips for New Ministers

John Killinger

Sharing years of wisdom from more than fifty years in ministry and teaching, *The Ministry Life: 101 Tips for New Ministers* by John Killinger is filled with practical advice and wisdom for a minister's day-to-day tasks as well as advice on intellectual and spiritual habits to keep ministers of any age healthy and fulfilled.   *978-1-57312-662-5 244 pages/pb* **$19.00**

To order call **1-800-747-3016** or visit **www.helwys.com**

Mount and Mountain
Vol. 1: A Reverend and a Rabbi Talk About the Ten Commandments
Rami Shapiro and Michael Smith

Mount and Mountain represents the first half of an interfaith dialogue—a dialogue that neither preaches nor placates but challenges its participants to work both singly and together in the task of reinterpreting sacred texts. Mike and Rami discuss the nature of divinity, the power of faith, the beauty of myth and story, the necessity of doubt, the achievements, failings, and future of religion, and, above all, the struggle to live ethically and in harmony with the way of God.   *978-1-57312-612-0 144 pages/pb* **$15.00**

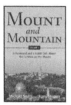

Mount and Mountain
Vol. 2: A Reverend and a Rabbi Talk About the Sermon on the Mount
Rami Shapiro and Michael Smith

This book, focused on the Sermon on the Mount, represents the second half of Mike and Rami's dialogue. In it, Mike and Rami explore the text of Jesus' sermon cooperatively, contributing perspectives drawn from their lives and religious traditions and seeking moments of illumination.   *978-1-57312-654-0 254 pages/pb* **$19.00**

Overcoming Adolescence
Growing Beyond Childhood into Maturity
Marion D. Aldridge

In *Overcoming Adolescence*, Marion Aldridge poses questions for adults of all ages to consider. His challenge to readers is one he has personally worked to confront: to grow up *all the way*—mentally, physically, academically, socially, emotionally, and spiritually. The key involves not only knowing how to work through the process but also how to recognize what may be contributing to our perpetual adolescence.

978-1-57312-577-2 156 pages/pb **$17.00**

Psychic Pancakes & Communion Pizza
More Musings and Mutterings of a Church Misfit
Bert Montgomery

Psychic Pancakes & Communion Pizza is Bert Montgomery's highly anticipated follow-up to *Elvis, Willie, Jesus & Me* and contains further reflections on music, film, culture, life, and finding Jesus in the midst of it all.   *978-1-57312-578-9 160 pages/pb* **$16.00**

Quiet Faith

An Introvert's Guide to Spiritual Survival

Judson Edwards

In eight finely crafted chapters, Edwards look at key issues like evangelism, interpreting the Bible, dealing with doubt, and surviving the church from the perspective of a confirmed, but sometimes reluctant, introvert. In the process, he offers some provocative insights that introverts will find helpful and reassuring.   *978-1-57312-681-6 144 pages/pb* **$15.00**

Reading Ezekiel (Reading the Old Testament series)

A Literary and Theological Commentary

Marvin A. Sweeney

The book of Ezekiel points to the return of YHWH to the holy temple at the center of a reconstituted Israel and creation at large. As such, the book of Ezekiel portrays the purging of Jerusalem, the Temple, and the people, to reconstitute them as part of a new creation at the conclusion of the book. With Jerusalem, the Temple, and the people so purged, YHWH stands once again in the holy center of the created world.

978-1-57312-658-8 264 pages/pb **$22.00**

Reading Job (Reading the Old Testament series)

A Literary and Theological Commentary

James L. Crenshaw

At issue in the Book of Job is a question with which most all of us struggle at some point in life, "Why do bad things happen to good people?" James Crenshaw has devoted his life to studying the disturbing matter of theodicy—divine justice—that troubles many people of faith.

978-1-57312-574-1 192 pages/pb **$22.00**

Reading Judges (Reading the Old Testament series)

A Literary and Theological Commentary

Mark E. Biddle

Reading the Old Testament book of Judges presents a number of significant challenges related to social contexts, historical settings, and literary characteristics. Acknowledging and examining these difficulties provides a point of entry into the world of Judges and promises to enrich the reading experience.   *978-1-57312-631-1 240 pages/pb* **$22.00**

Reading Samuel (Reading the Old Testament series)
A Literary and Theological Commentary
Johanna W. H. van Wijk-Bos

Interpreted masterfully by preeminent Old Testament scholar Johanna W. H. van Wijk-Bos, the story of Samuel touches on a vast array of subjects that make up the rich fabric of human life. The reader gains an inside look at leadership, royal intrigue, military campaigns, occult practices, and the significance of religious objects of veneration.

978-1-57312-607-6 *272 pages/pb* **$22.00**

The Role of the Minister in a Dying Congregation
Lynwood B. Jenkins

Jenkins provides a courageous and responsible resource on one of the most critical issues in congregational life: how to help a congregation conclude its ministry life cycle with dignity and meaning.

978-1-57312-571-0 *96 pages/pb* **$14.00**

Sessions with Genesis (Session Bible Studies series)
The Story Begins
Tony W. Cartledge

Immersing us in the book of Genesis, Tony Cartledge examines both its major stories and the smaller cycles of hope and failure, of promise and judgment. Genesis introduces these themes of divine faithfulness and human failure in unmistakable terms, tracing Israel's beginning to the creation of the world and professing a belief that Israel's particular history had universal significance.

978-1-57312-636-6 *144 pages/pb* **$14.00**

Sessions with Philippians (Session Bible Studies series)
Finding Joy in Community
Bo Prosser

In this brief letter to the Philippians, Paul makes clear the centrality of his faith in Jesus Christ, his love for the Philippian church, and his joy in serving both Christ and their church.

978-1-57312-579-6 *112 pages/pb* **$13.00**

Sessions with Samuel (Session Bible Studies series)
Stories from the Edge
Tony W. Cartledge

In these stories, Israel faces one crisis after another, a people constantly on the edge. Individuals such as Saul and David find themselves on the edge as well, facing troubles of leadership and personal struggle. Yet, each crisis becomes a gateway for learning that God is always present, that hope remains.

978-1-57312-555-0 *112 pages/pb* **$13.00**

Silver Linings
My Life Before and After Challenger 7

June Scobee Rodgers

We know the public story of *Challenger 7*'s tragic destruction. That day, June's life took a new direction that ultimately led to the creation of the Challenger Center and to new life and new love. Her story of Christian faith and triumph over adversity will inspire readers of every age. *978-1-57312-570-3 352 pages/hc* **$28.00**

Spacious
Exploring Faith and Place

Holly Sprink

Exploring where we are and why that matters to God is an ongoing process. If we are present and attentive, God creatively and continuously widens our view of the world, whether we live in the Amazon or in our own hometown. *978-1-57312-649-6 156 pages/pb* **$16.00**

This Is What a Preacher Looks Like
Sermons by Baptist Women in Ministry

Pamela Durso, ed.

In this collection of sermons by thirty-six Baptist women, their voices are soft and loud, prophetic and pastoral, humorous and sincere. They are African American, Asian, Latina, and Caucasian. They are sisters, wives, mothers, grandmothers, aunts, and friends.

978-1-57312-554-3 144 pages/pb **$18.00**

Transformational Leadership
Leading with Integrity

Charles B. Bugg

"Transformational" leadership involves understanding and growing so that we can help create positive change in the world. This book encourages leaders to be willing to change if *they* want to help transform the world. They are honest about their personal strengths and weaknesses, and are not afraid of doing a fearless moral inventory of themselves.

978-1-57312-558-1 112 pages/pb **$14.00**

Made in the USA
Columbia, SC
26 June 2022